Otto Pollak

. . . called "the senior author" in these pages, is professor of Sociology at the University of Pennsylvania. He holds a Doctorate of Law from the University of Vienna, an M.A. Degree from Bryn Mawr College, and a Ph.D. from the University of Pennsylvania. He has been a member of the Advisory Committee for the Aging, the Governor's Office, Commonwealth of Pennsylvania, and a Fellow of the Philadelphia College of Physicians. In a long and active career he has published more than seventy-five professional articles or books.

Nancy L. Kelley

. . . is a Director of Studies at the Baldwin School, Bryn Mawr, Pennsylvania. She holds a B.A. Degree from Chestnut Hill College, an M.A. Degree from Bryn Mawr College, and a Ph.D. in Social Science from the Medical College of Pennsylvania.

THE
Challenges of Aging

THE
Challenges of Aging

BY
Otto Pollak & Nancy L. Kelley

NORTH RIVER PRESS

Library of Congress Cataloging in Publication Data
Pollak, Otto, 1908-
    The challenges of aging.

    Bibliography: p.
    1. Old age—United States.   2. Aging
I. Kelley, Nancy L., 1950-   joint author.
II. Title
HQ1064.U5P63   305.2′6   80-27600
ISBN 0-88427-045-9

PERMISSIONS

The excerpt on pages 108-111 is from Robert Peck, "Psychological Developments in the Second Half of Life," in Joan E. Anderson, ed., *Psychological Aspects of Aging* (Washington, D.C.: American Psychological Association, 1956), pp. 46-48. Copyright 1956 by the American Psychological Association. Reprinted by permission.

Manufactured in the United States of America

Dedication

To those whom we love
and from who we have learned.

Contents

Introduction

Old age is the longest stage of development in the life of an individual. Life in advancing years may actually cover three decades. In recent times medical advances have helped people to look forward to constantly increasing years of life. Since the changes of that period of life are frequently losses, the life task of people in that age group is the development of successful adaptations and compensations. A study of religion, philosophy and modern psychology shows that there are some distinct themes in these efforts to cope.

Persistent among them is the idea of a gradual withdrawal from activities. The well-known "disengagement theory" suggests that people and their younger associates engage in a reciprocal process of withdrawal from one another. Mandatory retirement is an example of the withdrawal of the working world from its members; early retirement is an example of withdrawal of the old from their younger associates.

The concept of disengagement covers two totally different forms of experience. The one is rejection and the other is self-preservation. Although, like every other experience, both forms of disengagement are conflicted, only voluntary withdrawal has the connotation of self-preservation by restoring harmony between one's capacities and the demands one has to meet. A professional does not have to compete with people more recently trained. A wall painter does not have to climb ladders anymore. A person does not have to go out in the evenings for committee meetings or parties. The disengaged life, however, will be a successful life only for those who have either religious, philosophical, or inner resources to help them tolerate the lack of outside relationships so that they do not become subject to anxiety or depression.

We will mention in the course of this book that the greatest comfort of religion in old age is the belief in a life after death. A religious attitude, however, is more than just this belief. It is the acceptance of the will of God, whether expressed in a prayer as "Thy will be done," in a belief in Kismet, or in the words of Job after his many trials from the Lord, "The Lord gave, and the Lord hath taken away; blessed be the name of the Lord (1:21-22)." Even if aging is experienced only as a series of losses, a religious attitude of acceptance will see the aged through.

For those who need ego support from others, disengagement will not work. It is for this reason that many experts on aging advocate continued activities in advancing years. This can occur on the level of community service, or service to relatives and friends; and on the level of leisure it can occur through such activities as visits to museums, ritualized luncheons with friends, memberships in clubs and senior citizen centers, or going every morning to the public library to read the newspapers. Perhaps the most meaningful of such activities is serving as volunteers in hospitals. Here is an activity which combines usefulness to society with ego affirmation and defense against anxiety. It also brings structure to unstructured time, facilitates new contacts and protects against the feeling of segregation from people in other age groups. Most important, doing volunteer work provides opportunities to exercise one's mind or body and prevents decline of capacities by non-use.

Another theory of adaptation in old age suggests that people really do not change much. Active people remain active in old age. Passive people remain passive. Introverts remain introverts, and extroverts remain extroverts. The adaptive quality in this approach is the feeling of not being changed by advancing time. In a sense, if one remains virtually the same, one feels almost indestructible. This is tremendously helpful when one's body is constantly threatened by ailments of one sort or another. Personality in aging can work for you, with you or against you. Obviously, passive people will have a personality which smooths the road into old age. Passivity will also make the ultimately unavoidable dependency of old age an agreeable condition rather than an insult to self.

Active people, on the other hand, will have to cope with a personality that works against the aging process. They will remain active at the risk of health, becoming overtired and vulnerable to infections and high blood pressure. They will have to remain stoic about the discomforts which an aging body inflicts upon them. Their personality may spare them the experience of being diminished by time or by custodial care, however, and it may protect them against senility by keeping their minds alive. It will also reassure younger people about old age in this activity-centered world. When a woman in her seventies says that she is a volunteer in a hospital, has three Board memberships, two luncheon meetings per week with friends, and goes to the orchestra once a week, people are delighted and assured about their own future in old age.

A dangerous psychological attitude toward aging is the wish of some people to do or accomplish before the end what they missed out on while they were young and middle-aged. It is not likely that one will succeed in writing a great novel if one has never tried writing a short story. It is pathetic for people who have had demanding lives to go about in advanced years chasing "fun," or seeking a rich sex life after having led a rather puritanical existence. The modern philosophy of Existentialism can be seductive and misleading in this respect. Its emphasis on the human search for authenticity leads many people to make changes that their relatives and friends do not expect.

In contrast to this, there is an attitude of fulfillment and completion which may sustain one in old age. Every life is a fragment in terms of what one wanted to do. There are books to be read, places to go, friendships which one has not had the leisure to cultivate. Reading or re-reading the Bible from end to end may prove to be a ceaselessly flowing source of mental health. No matter which psychological approach to aging one chooses, the overriding psychological attitude which one needs in aging is courage. To pick oneself up after illness, to return from the funeral of a friend, not to become afraid of taking a trip and, finally, not to be afraid of being alone, require an ever-new commitment to life by a daily exercise of courage. This is courage which needs no public acclaim. Its exercise is certain to give satisfaction and a feeling of beauty to the self of the aging person.

This is the essential meaning of our book and its title, "The Challenges of Aging." It is easy to be attractive when one is young. But, as a famous Swiss writer once said, youth conceals ugliness. The aged have no such cover, and they must create the aesthetics of their particular stage of life. They can do this by meeting its challenges, by recourse to religion and philosophy, and by adapting with dignity, courage, and inventiveness, to live in harmony with their personality and their own experience of aging.

1

Time: Working For You, With You, or Against You?

The experience of aging and the prospect of dying evoke in human beings a concern with two great uncertainties. Most older people wonder when they will die and what, if anything, they will experience after death. In this and the following chapter we shall discuss the experience of these uncertainties. In the third chapter we shall present philosophical guidelines for coping with the anxieties which these uncertainties create.

Is an individual's life unique? Once finished, can it be started again? Can it be repeated, or at least be revived in different forms? These questions have preoccupied religious thinkers and philosophers from antiquity to the present. According to the approaches they used, they have offered different answers to the question of how to cope with aging and dying.

To the early Church Fathers life was the only test available to qualify a person for a specific type of life after death. To a Buddhist the life of the soul continued. According to its merits, a soul might be reborn at a higher or lower level than that of its previous existence. Only completeness of merit would lead a human being into Nirvana, the final state transcending suffering. To the Christian the

Sermon on the Mount expressed a similar belief: "Blessed are the poor in spirit for theirs is the kingdom of Heaven."

Epicurus (c. 300 B.C.), the founder of Hedonism, said it is the uniqueness of the human experience which distinguishes it from other living phenomena in nature. The moon waxes and wanes in endless repetition, trees lose their leaves in the fall and bring forth new ones in the spring. Humans are different from these other forms of existence. They do not know seasonality. They are born as a result of a genetic accident, grow from infancy to adulthood, and then decline until death. Once they die, the results of their birth begin to disappear; the body returns to nature. Just because of this lack of recurrence, Epicurus saw human life as the only value over which an individual has power and which one must therefore exhaust as one's unique possession. This theme appears over and over in philosophical and religious writings. Apparently, anyone facing the phenomenon of death is forced to ask whether the end of life is what it appears to be, whether it is definitive or transitional. Is it the end or a beginning? This is the ultimate enigma. Whether death is followed by decomposition or another life, surely in the here and now it is unique.

To Heidegger, the outstanding representative of the modern philosophy of existentialism, humanity is bounded by the temporality of human life, its limitation in time, and the dread of nothingness which looms at the end. We are born into a certain place in life, as a stone is thrown into the water. We spend our lives in a more or less conscious protest against the consequences of our birth. Even though we can make history, we have no choice into what period of history we will be born. We must live with the consequence of chance: the color, occupation, religion or status of our parents, the schools to which we are sent, the occupations for which we are prepared, and to a large extent, the society within which we interact with others.

We were placed in the world, but we must try to make or find our own place. From being wrong within the world, we must seek a life that gives us a feeling of being right. We must do all this against the threat of not having enough time. This feeling of urgency makes many of us exhausted, despondent, and depressed before the end. And the aged person experiences the feelings of urgency and depression more than the young.

Over a span of more than two thousand years of recorded time, and over a space reaching from east to west, it appears that humans have always been concerned with the apparent limitations of the life span, and with the question of extending life into another form. If life is considered finite, then time, like the two-faced god Janus, looks forward and backward. Children look forward. They are impatient with time and want to grow up. Old people, on the other hand, seem to look backward. They like to reminisce; they consider childhood wistfully as a golden age which will never be theirs again. Psychologically, they drag their feet. But even when old people say that the old times were the best, they also admit that if they could live their lives over again, they would do things differently.

Apparently, people reminisce about the good things and tend to forget the bad. What one tells about one's past is probably pleasure, achievement, and victory or rescue from disaster. Reminiscing seems, therefore, to be selective.

Refugees from concentration camps may reminisce on their escape, their survival, but they rarely reminisce about having been tortured or about having lost spouses or children in gas chambers. Instead people tend to fantasize about what they could have done differently in the past. Although this appears to be a meaningless exercise because the past is beyond our power to change, it has therapeutic value for many people.

It is said that when Zenon (c.300 B.C.), the founder of the Stoics, broke his toe, he beat the earth and said, "Why are you calling, I am coming," and went home and killed himself. Though probably few Stoics would respond this way today, they do believe in and accept the temporality of life. The laws of life — to them — are in harmony with the laws of nature. Stoicism is a somewhat somber philosophy, accepting but not enjoying natural law.

Until recently, people have been spared too much preoccupation with aging and dying. Death came to them relatively early, through battle, childbirth, or disease. To reach the biblical three-score-and-ten was indeed a distinction making up for the infirmities and sufferings which accompanied advanced years. But now many people live into their seventies and eighties and have as much as twenty or thirty years in which they experience physiological and social decline. They have lost the distinction of survivorship. In many instances, they have become a burden to themselves and to society, without losing the wish to continue life. It could be said, therefore, that the young are ungrateful optimists and the old are grateful pessimists. This, however, would be an overstatement because children experience many moments of exhilaration, and old people finally turn the wish to live into the wish to die. The young have both time and hope, though they may not appreciate them. The old have less of both, but still hang on to what is left. Only toward the end do they lose their will to live.

Generally speaking, every phase of life has its own comforts and discomforts. Children have the effortless, but to them, apparently endless experience of maturation. They do not have to work for their organic growth. Short of maltreatment by parents or caretakers, it just happens. They gain mobility, height, strength; they become "more." And throughout this process of growth, they fight internal and external limitations.

Older people, on the other hand, experience the opposite process, involution. They lose mobility, size, strength, and they become weaker, more brittle, and less acute in their physical senses. Only when life has no more comforts at all, only when there are no more victories of adaptation to the difficulties of decline, are people ready to die. Then they are probably instrumental in bringing death about, by refusing to help physicians, nurses, technicians, and anybody who wants to keep them alive.

From infancy through adolescence human beings experience the excitement or consolation — no matter how conflicted — of physiological maturation. They experience an increase of ability to cope with internal and environmental challenges, new information, and freedom from the limitations of childhood and education. In maturity the body goes through a process of decline which between the ages of twenty and thirty is hardly noticed, between thirty and forty is noticed with a degree of amusement, and only later creates a measure of apprehension. While this decline occurs in the physical realm, there is still social advancement in the economic sphere and in the experience of familial life.

Up to middle age and beyond, time works for one. It makes one strong, it widens one's range of experience and it gives one the illusion of fulfillment. Having children often gives the impression of a harvest and of fulfilled adulthood, no matter how many demands children may make, how much worry they arouse, and how rarely they do what their parents want them to do. If children get married and have children in turn, they give their parents a feeling of biological perpetuity which balances, at least temporarily, the feeling of being "over the hill."

Only when social decline joins physiological decline is time beginning to work unequivocally aginst one. Sensory perceptions begin to fail, retirement looms for women and for men. Time holds fewer and fewer promises of bailing out one's mistakes.

Frequently, people in their sixties, feeling the loss of time, take expensive trips "while they are still healthy." They get divorces to have another chance at marriage, or they try second careers, "while there is still time." Actually, however, their basic preoccupation is shifting from living to death and dying. The physician who ends a checkup with the expressed or implied statement, "good for another year," does little to help the patient refocus on life.

Childhood is beset with fears and with the irritation resulting from limiting care by older persons. It is disturbed by anxiety over failure, and it is exposed to any number of hazards in development. Children in our society are adored and catered to. Their parents give inordinate amounts of money for their education and for material luxuries. They put up with the insufferable egotism of adolescence. And yet, their children look terribly unhappy. Adults are bewildered that so many of the young people resort to drugs in order to change their state of consciousness, and that some go so far as to become terrorists. Parental helplessness, when faced with such expressions of revolt and despair, is one of the tragedies of our time. It would seem that just the abundance of time does not make living easy or happy.

Similarly, one will find old people who suffer from painful arthritis, who are unable to read without developing double vision, and who can't hear without asking their associates to raise their voices. There are those who must take medication against high blood pressure, those who have had to undergo surgery for cancer, those whose equanimity is over and over interrupted by the anxiety created by medical tests. And yet, many of these people seem to enjoy life; they seem able to amuse themselves on a day-to-day basis.

The famous French author Simone de Beauvoir described the feeling of liberation which can come to the aged as a result of having to slow down, and she asked a question: "Since every qualification is at the same time a limitation, might it not be supposed that in losing his qualifications the individual finds the world more open to him?" Old people may have more time for doing things they always wanted to do, and, before they become too incapacitated, they may decide to pursue the pleasures which were either out of their reach or seemed too "self-centered" to engage in.

Old people slow down, they need more time to get up, to fix breakfast, to clean house, to write letters, see doctors, write checks, and make the bank statements balance. And they need rest in between. The fact that they slow down may help to keep time from becoming empty. Furthermore, it may make the small acts of daily life more meaningful.

Perhaps the most rewarding aspect of time at that stage in life is rest. Declining capabilities and loss of vitality make for recurrent fatigue. Recuperation requires rest, rest requires time, and in that sense time works for the older person by reviving and maintaining his or her strength.

The quality of hope changes as the meaning of the moment changes. For the young, unless it is exceptionally happy or exceptionally unhappy, the moment is part of the routine of living, for the aged person who wants to live, every moment is an event. The simple fact that one has lived to experience it makes it "momentous."

Young people may hope to lead a meaningful life, to be successful even at some cost, and ultimately to find clarity in their lives. The hopes of older people are more limited by the time they have left. For this reason, their responses are less wide-ranging but nonetheless life-sustaining. Where a young person may want to be a great poet, a great scientist or a business tycoon, an older person may hope to be able to maintain good health, or the current status of living. He or she may desire only to find some relief from pain, to live until a cure for cancer has been found, or just to be able to wake up the next morning. Not even major writers, painters or scientists are likely to start a series of novels, paintings or research projects in the expectation of seeing them to their conclusion. The hopes of older people tend to be much more modest. For example, the senior author remembers a conversation with a well-known psychoanalyst about academic life in the last year before retirement. She mentioned that she had repeatedly to turn down suggestions from her colleagues to apply to the National Institute of Mental Health for "five" year research grants.

Since living consumes time, time works for us only if we use it. The Chinese have a proverb that thought which leads to a decision is wasted if the decision is not carried out. Actually, one can say that every phase of life is wasted if it is not fully lived, if its potential is not realized. And often, when the consequences of the decision are mulled over before carrying it out, the time for enjoying its fruits has to some degree passed. In reality decisions are often made too late.

Freud called the postponement of fulfillment an expression of maturity and placed the "reality" principle over the "pleasure" principle in human development. This suggests that one should sacrifice the pleasure of the moment for the pleasure of the future, and should prepare oneself for the future. However, it overlooks the changes that occur in the situation and in the person in the process of arriving at a decision. The person who wants to wait until he or she is perfectly ready will never be ready, because time not used is time lost.

For this reason many people, who in the eyes of the world have been successful, are unhappy in their old age, regretting the pleasures they have forsaken, the times they have taken from being with family or friends in order to be in conferences or at work in their offices. Unless time is used in ways that feel "authentic" or good, there will be regret.

Hope does not disappear with time. In old age it changes content and becomes more moderate, more accompanied by regrets over what one cannot do anymore. However, it persists much longer than young people expect or understand. If and when hope disappears, people become ready to die. Since dying is a necessity, becoming ready for it — not looking to time anymore with hope — may be an ultimate boon of aging. Time and hope are inseparable. When hope disappears, time comes to an end.

2

The Dread of Nothingness and the Belief in a Life After Death

As far as we know, people have always been afraid of death. Throughout history people have sought to remove all visible signs of death from any easily accessible place. The Second Law of the Twele Tables of ancient Rome says, "Do not bury the dead in or near the cities," and to this day local legislation seeks to keep cemeteries out of the cities. One interesting exception to this custom is the Woodland Avenue cemetery in Philadelphia, which lies adjacent to the Veterans Hospital.

The fear of death is built into a tradition and used by society in many different ways. The most serious crimes, such as murder or treason, are punishable by death. It is not death as such but its closeness and the knowledge of the exact hour which is the essence of this punishment. The human skeleton is a symbol of death, reminding us of the end and the decay of the flesh. The fact that the skeleton is used at halloween for fun suggests a denial of anxiety over death and an initiation rite for young children in confronting its effects. In the Middle Ages, the human skeleton was frequently used as a reminder of the punishment one could expect for evil done during life. To this day, we are reminded of the origin and the end of organic life by the ritual statement on Ash Wednesday, the first day of Lent, "Remember, man, that thou art dust and unto dust thou shalt return." When Roman Catholics wear the mark of ashes on their foreheads on that day, we are all reminded of the omnipresence of death.

Only in rare instances is death seen at all as positive and enhancing to the person. Two notable examples of this are death as a religious martyr, or death in the defense of one's country. And even in the case of martyrs and heroes, death has always been an occasion for mourning and sorrow for the survivors. Suicide is also, to be sure, an exercise in autonomy over one's life and death, but hardly anyone ever got a monument or a commendation for taking his or her own life.

In almost every respect, death is visualized as the opposite of birth. We have no way of knowing whether the foetus has an expectation of being born while it is still *in utero*. On the other hand, almost everyone who is born expects to die and, at one time or another, is afraid of dying. This expectation is with young people in combat, with adults during serious illness, and with old people also as an increasing preoccupation and immediate concern without specific illness. The marriage vow is frequently taken with the words "until death do us part," and people try to provide for spouse and progeny even after death by making wills and establishing trusts.

Wills and trusts express two things: the evaluation of oneself as capable and adequate in financial matters, and the evaluation of others as needing financial care by somebody more competent than they are. They also connote a wish to perpetuate, if not life, then at least power. So, the wish to extend one's influence beyond life may be either benevolent or self-centered. The effectiveness of such effort is, however, always subject to change. People to whom one leaves bequests may die before you, trusts may have to change beneficiaries, and sometimes — as Shakespeare showed so many years ago in *King Lear* — the recipients of one's caring may be too blindly or hastily chosen.

The preoccupation with the material effects of dying shields us from a direct confrontation with death. Planning for future largess gives people power beyond the absolutely helpless state of death. People hope to be remembered in this way. They establish foundations and bequeath funds for charitable or educational buildings which will carry their name, or at least the family name, long after their death.

Ironically, foundations and bequests often fail the purpose of the donor. Every university is full of buildings named after people who are long forgotten. The portraits of politicians and professors in libraries and faculty clubs are looked at rarely and without emotion or remembrance. In recent times even the busts of people who are as well-known historically as Lincoln, Emerson, Thoreau and Whitman are at risk of having to be relocated from the Hall of Fame for financial reasons. *Sic transit gloria mundi* — So passes the glory of the world.

This very helplessness to influence the lives of others after death, and this failure to be remembered, reveals the essential characteristics of the end of life: it may be postponed but it cannot be avoided. Regrettably, those who are usually remembered in history are those who have caused others to die prematurely: Caesar, Genghis Khan, Napoleon, Hitler, to name only a few. It is interesting that the benefactors of humanity are more quickly forgotten than its torturers, as Gibbon has pointed out.

Every human being is afraid of the unknown, although the unknown may also hold a chance for the better. Death is dreadful because it is unknown and outside the reach of experience. Children and young people overcome the fear of the unknown by the assuring experience of maturation and the fulfillment of their expectations. For aging people there is no such support. They connect aging with the experience of loss. As years go by, they fear their losses will become larger and larger, and that at some point they will be unable to function. Time confirms these fears, it doesn't eliminate them. To quote Simone de Beauvoir once again,

> Even if the old person is struck by no particular misfortune (physical suffering, outliving all those one loves), he has usually either lost his reasons for living or he has discovered their absence. The reason why death fills us with anxiety is that it is the inescapable reverse of our projects: . . . But for man living means self-transcendence. A consequence of biological decay is the impossibility of surpassing oneself and of becoming passionately concerned with anything; it kills all projects, and it is by this expedient that it renders death acceptable.

When we face senility, we fear losing our mind, we fear losing what we still value most in us, whatever beauty our body still has. Facing death, we fear losing the ultimate value, ourselves.

And still the fear of dying is mingled with hope. Cicero said that "no one is so old as to think that he cannot live one more year." The unknown, therefore, is also a condition of hope. The Scriptures tell us that man's life is three-score-ten, or four score at best, and, if it has been excellent, it has been full of labor and pain. That part of life which we have lived contains many things which we would prefer not to have happened to us. The part of life that we have not yet lived is the harbor of hope. The past is usually seen as unsatisfactory when compared with "the way things might have been." What keeps people going apparently is not so much what has happened to them but what they hope they will yet experience. Death is the exception to this, however. Death is the sum of the two greatest burdens of man: the combination of helplessness and hopelessness.

For this reason, people have tried to believe in a life after death. This is probably most strongly expressed in the concept of heaven and hell, and in the idea of purgatory where one "cleanses the soul" before entering heaven. The Mohammedan idea of life after death is one of sensual happiness. The Christian idea makes heaven a non-sensual or at least a non-sexual condition of happiness. Angels have wings but they do not have genitalia. Whatever cultural projection the notions of life after death may present, they seem to be wish fulfillment seen from an earthly perspective.

The content of life after death is always seen as dependent on the life one has led before death. The sinner will go to hell, and the good person will go to heaven. The Catholic concept of absolution gives the sinner a chance to go to heaven by gaining God's forgiveness through repentance and the ministrations of a priest. The Buddhist who lives a good life will be reborn in a higher form of physical state. The idea of life after death is therefore connected with the idea of God. It implies the existence and effectiveness of a supernatural power, or of two supernatural powers: good and evil, with humanity the battlefield between the two.

Belief in the life after death is unavoidably connected with the idea that the conduct of life directs people into a specific condition after death. An ethical conduct of life is worshipping God, an unethical one is worshipping the devil. To believe in a life after death, therefore, does not always mean to believe in a desirable existence. However, in humanity's need for immortality, probably any form of life after death seems better than no life.

Unfortunately there are older people who lose their faith by asking God for exception from the laws of creation. To ask that one's spouse may not die from a terminal disease or to ask that one may not be subjected to the infirmities of aging is ultimately to ask God to be treated as an exception, and it dooms the petitioner to disappointment. To believe is to yield to God.

For people who have no belief in God or the devil, the problem of death is one of discontinuity. As Heidegger put it, it is the dread of nothingness in life, the irrevocable progression toward its end. This raises an ethical problem: how can one live without hope? Heidegger would say that one must reduce hope from the infinite to the finite, from a long-range to a short-range point of view. People must shift wish fulfillment from an endless perspective of time to one which is limited but not fully known, to one which is uncertain in content and length but certain in being finite. For the existentialist, who believes that people have all suffered lack of feeling right in the world by being thrown into life, the hope is for an authentic life someday before death.

David Reisman, a famous sociologist speaking in the existentialist mood, says, "... allowing a person to be confronted for a time with nothingness might save him — or destroy him — depending on what inner resources he could muster to the challenge." People like to be certain; they want to know the date of major events in their lives, such as weddings, commencements, promotions, meetings, and when children or spouses are coming home. Only for death do we need and crave the uncertainty of timing. And for most of us this culmination of hopelessness and helplessness remains hidden from our sight at some unknown point in the future.

3

Three Philosophical Perspectives on Aging and Dying

For those who do not have the comfort of religion, philosophy is an important source of strength in coping with the losses which the experience of aging invariably implies. A modern social gerontologist, Donald Kent, says, "The lack of a philosophy of life which offers psychic compensation for the decrements of age, the lack in our social structure of formal institutional supports for the transitions in the later parts of the life cycle, and the lack of empathy and respect for those who have aged are more serious deficiencies than the lack of adequate material comforts."

Although there are probably as many philosophies as there are philosophers, we have chosen to view aging, dying, and death from the viewpoint of only three philosophies. We do this because Stoicism, Hedonism and Existentialism have dealt extensively with these topics, and because they seem to furnish guidelines of behavior which are applicable today.

STOICISM

For Zenon, the founder of Stoicism, philosophy was not dead knowledge but the search and recognition of the shaping forces in life and their application in human conduct. Philosophy was the teacher of the art of living. Stoicism sees life as a series of obligations which one must fulfill without complaining. It has been said that Zenon was of Jewish origin. Possibly his acquaintance with the Jewish religion, which is essentially a body of rules for human conduct, led him to the development of his philosophy. Although his school flourished in Athens where he lived, it had powerful competition there. In Rome, however, Stoicism had great impact on public life. There it was represented by Seneca, Epictetus, and the Emperor Marcus Aurelius, all leading figures of their time.

Stoics were found among rulers and subjects. For the former, Stoicism represented a commitment to assume the burdens of public office and to carry them out without rebellion against the sacrifice of leisure and personal comfort which they demanded. For the subjects, though, Stoicism was a support in suffering subjugation, or a means of escape from it. Suicide was acceptable to Stoics. They saw it as a road to freedom providing solace to those who dared to defy a Roman Emperor.

Stoicism assumed that the laws of nature applied to all human beings. This led to the development of a body of laws believed to be applicable to all people. The practical use of natural law helped Roman administrators to govern people of such diversity as Britons and Greeks, Germans and Spaniards, Celts and Egyptians. It is a principle still active today in international politics regarding human rights.

Stoics were not persons bent on obtaining pleasure and avoiding pain. They were stern, self-contained persons who accepted and fulfilled destiny in terms of what they perceived to be natural law.

Marcus Aurelius, the Emperor and Stoic, addressed people with the following statement, "Thou hast embarked, thou hast made the voyage, thou art come to the shore; get out. If indeed to another life, there is no want of gods, not even there. But if to a state without sensation, thou wilt cease to be held by pains and pleasure, and to be a slave to the vessel, which is as much inferior as that which serves it is superior: for the one is intelligence and deity; the other is earth and corruption."

For Stoics aging and dying spelled liberation from a fate which they suffered and tried to fulfill without complaint. For them life was not to be enjoyed for its pleasures. The only satisfaction it afforded was the sense of enjoyment from acting in harmony with natural law. To have done one's duty, to have suffered silently, to be delivered by death from the burden of living were the only positive experiences available within this philosophical approach.

Much as one must admire the logic of Stoicism and its applicability to the problems of old age, one cannot help but feel that this attitude toward death and dying was a philosophy for middle-aged members of the governing class for whom public presentation of self was of overriding importance. It was formulated by people still in possession of their powers, not burdened by years of physiological deterioration, by physical pain, and by the fear of death. It was developed at a period of history when few people lived to be seventy years or older.

It is unlikely that in our time there would be many people who would find it congenial to apply this philosophy. This is not an age in which people accept natural law without protest. Technological and medical advances encourage the opposite. The spirit of our civilization is not favorable to such preparation for aging. The temper of our time demands immediate gratification, searches for the fulfillment of fantasies, and escape from burdens of life and age.

Still there may be people to whom a Stoic stance toward life would appeal. Since our schools do not teach us how to be Stoic, such people would have to prepare themselves for Stoicism in old age. One way of doing so would be to start experimenting with roleplaying of Stoic responses to what happens to them. For example, a Stoic would suffer the loss of a spouse without withdrawing from the activities that he or she formerly pursued. He or she would take retirement without resentment, and physical pain as a challenge to show fortitude. People who try such Stoicism will find that their behavior will produce the corresponding psychological reactions of tolerance for loss and suffering.

HEDONISM

A second philosophy, Hedonism, was founded by Epicurus. In many respects it is the opposite of the teaching of Zenon and his Roman followers.

Epicurus saw the key to understanding human behavior in the pursuit of pleasure and the avoidance of pain. However, since pleasure is usually followed by pain, as everyone knows who has fallen in love, acquired property or held public office, this is life as it is. It is not life as it should be. Thus Epicurus was led to advocate a tensionless life in which neither passion nor desire would rule. He counseled escape from the demands of a political or even a familial life, and he saw in the pursuit of philosophy the highest, and at the same time, the most painless conduct for human beings. In psychoanalytic terms, he counseled restriction of the ego as the most satisfactory way of avoiding the pains which seem to be so often connected with the pursuit of pleasure.

His teachings have frequently been misinterpreted as a philosophy which extols the seeking of pleasure. In reality it is a system more suited to a monk than to the average person. Strangely enough, both the true teaching of Epicurus, as well as the misinterpretation of them, would seem to fit aging more easily than the teaching of Stoics. Since old people are frequently retired from business and removed from other activities such as sports because of failing strength, they are almost forced into the inconspicuous life which Epicurus advocates. Even when Hedonism is misinterpreted to be a life devoted to the pursuit of pleasure, the philosophy fits the opportunity of old people to free themselves from the burdensome responsibilities of adulthood. They do not have to commute to and from work. They do not have to keep office hours.

A recently retired person in the hills near Berkley, California, told the senior author in an interview that his greatest enjoyment was to have a relaxed breakfast with his wife while watching the morning rush hour traffic heading toward the Bay Bridge.

The old do not have to raise children any more. Time is theirs to take a walk when they want to, to sit when they want to, to chat with friends as long as they want to, to stay at home when others must rush to their offices. It could be liberation from a stressful life, liberation from the whip of ambition, from the claims of work and competition, possibly even from the claims of love.

An exception to this possible enjoyment of an undemanding life is the medical regimen which deprives older people of the "Hedonistic" pleasures of eating and drinking. Every medical checkup threatens older people with restrictions of their diet. They are not supposed to eat dark meat, nor to put salt on their food; they must limit their intake of liquids. One could almost say to an old person, "Every visit to a doctor diminishes you!"

Our society is inconsistent in helping older people to shift to an unobtrusive way of life. Old people who are busy in civic affairs as members of boards and committees, as volunteers in hospitals, and who continue to play tennis or golf, are commended for remaining in the stream of life. The sexual revolution, moreover, puts many older people into a bind by suggesting that sexual intercourse can and should be continued up into the 80's, overlooking for instance that many drugs against hypertension seem to have impotence as a side effect. Old people faced with such contradictions in the societal expectations which they must meet, must decide which of these expectations are in harmony with their philosophy and which are not.

Unfortunately, Epicurus made two psycological mistakes. He believed that a life without much input would lead to peace of mind, and he disregarded the fact that people, by and large, fear death no matter how much they are told that it is senseless to be afraid of being nothing. In reality, peace of mind can be achieved only the resolution of internal conflicts and freedom from death anxiety only by acceptance and not by intellectual argument. This reduces the number of old people who might benefit from a hedonistic way of life to those who, either through a fortunate childhood, or through therapy, have reached senescence more or less conflict-free, and who have accepted death as unavoidable. The hedonistic answer, of course, would be a conduct of life that would avoid exposure to failure or physical exhaustion. In other terms, disengagement rather than involvement would be the Epicurean answer to the problem of aging.

EXISTENTIALISM

Psychologically, Existentialism is the most realistic of the three philosophies that we are considering. In Heidegger's work the awareness of the limitations of human life, its temporality, and the "dread of nothingness," are identified as the crucial experiences of human existence. Life's limitation in time is in conflict with the discomfort that human beings experience as a result of having been thrown into life with consequences over which they have little or no control. We cannot help being born to live in the twentieth century. We cannot help being born to parents to live in a certain neighborhood which determines our schooling. And perhaps most of all, we cannot help pursuing occupations and becoming attached to mates as a result of our school experience. Lives which are led as a result of such experience are felt not to be "right." Heidegger calls the feeling of rightness in the world "authenticity," and he believes that many of us are searching for it by rebelling against the accidents of birth and their consequences. Because of its limitation in time, we experience a sense of urgency in the search for authenticity in life. Existentialism doesn't argue against the fear of death; it accepts it as an explanation of human life. it doesn't argue with human feelings about age and dying; instead it derives understanding from them.

The search for authenticity appeals to people in our time, expressing itself in the "do it," "seize the time" phrases of the sixties, in the "be real" and "drop out" subcultures of the sixties and seventies, and probably in the burgeoning numbers of people who divorce and remarry in the hope of "making a fresh start in life." However, existentialism may cause older people who follow it to act foolish. It may seduce people in advanced years into seeking a new way of life which they are not equipped to lead or to handle, and into letting go of their past values and identities.

Existentialism, though psychologically correct, is a philosophy only for relatively young people, because it emphasizes the importance of the self and of the present. On the other hand, a philosophy of life which minimizes the importance of the here and now can make decline or absence of capacities relatively unimportant. Stoicism and Hedonism, although psychologically wrong in their attempts to fight the fear of death, are both philosophies which can enable people to cope with aging. They promote a perspective in which the self is seen not as the center but only as a small — but not insignificant — item in the universe.

In summary, Stoicism may shorten the life of old people by leading them to continue carrying burdens and being involved, but there are psychological benefits in such involvement. Hedonism may preserve life by recommending a removal from its pressures and a passionless approach, but then what is life preserved for unless it be life itself? Existentialism may activate the zest for life by suggesting experimentation with alternatives, but creates the risk of failure and damage to the physical self and to the self-image. Which philosophy one chooses may have mostly to do with personality and not with reasoned decision making. A Kansas City Study of Adult Life proposed "that personality is the pivotal dimension in the various patterns of aging...." The question which philosophy is the "best," then, is not well formulated. Everybody must ask: what philosophy is best for me? Having found the answer, one will have to bring one's aging into harmony with it.

4

Children, Friends, and Strangers in the Perspective of Time

Confucius was once asked, "Is there one word which may serve as a rule of practice for all one's life?" He replied, "Is not reciprocity such a word?" The wisdom of the old Chinese philosopher still suggests the basic principle of satisfactory human relations. Human beings are open systems: they maintain themselves through exchanges.

The physiology of the mother and her newborn child is built for such exchanges. At birth the secretion of milk in the breast of the mother and the ability of the child to swallow prepare both for one of the most basic human exchanges, the exchange of nurture for love. The human physiognomy forces every human being to turn face to face with another for meaningful exchanges, or to turn away if he or she refuses. Language is probably the most powerful means of exchange. It can protect, comfort, assist, reassure, instruct, and strengthen human beings. Unfortunately it can also do the opposite. In fact, the polarity of human life can turn every opportunity for positive exchange into its opposite. Mothers can refuse to nurture their children, children can refuse nurture, the spoken word can wound, the touch can become a blow. Destruction can be exchanged for destruction, as well as support for support.

Our bodies both separate us from the rest of the world and connect us with it. Although our body surfaces bring gratification to others by touch and appearance, they are relatively less meaningful for life experience than our body openings. The mouth permits intake of food, the nose permits inhaling and exhaling of air and aromas, the rectum and urethra permit necessary elimination, the ears receive sound, the eyes accept visual images which orient us to presence and distance, to self and to others. The genital openings permit human beings our only, although illusive, experience of union and physical wholeness. These capacities for exchange diminish over time and what has been experienced almost as symbiosis changes to separation.

We experience many exchanges in the here and now. The child that is cradled by the mother receives and gives touch at the same time. The kiss of lovers or the sexual union gives immediate gratification. Also, less intimate interactions are usually experienced in such closeness of time that they seem to be immediate exchanges. Conversations occur in the present. Both the mere being together of good personal friends, and even the exchange of blows in physical fighting, have this quality of immediacy.

On the other hand, many exchanges occur over spans of time with one of the partners acting first and the other later. A loan is a perfect example of such an exchange. Money is given now and the repayment — if the lender is lucky — will occur later. Parents infuse nurture, support, and education into their children and expect to be rewarded by their appropriate development and, hopefully, by their gratitude and love, as well as by their support and nurture when they attain old age. It scarcely needs saying that one who fulfills his or her part of the exchange in the present and expects a return in the future is, in essence, a gambler, or at least an optimist who gives hostages to fortune. Nowhere has this been better expressed than in the advice of Polonius to his son Laertes in Shakespeare's *Hamlet:*

> *Neither a borrower nor a lender be:*
> *For a loan oft loses both itself and friend.*
> *(Act I, sc.3)*

Although many people who see *Hamlet* consider Polonius a fool, his advice to Laertes contains the wisdom of maturity, if not of old age.

The older one gets, the larger will grow one's experience of unpaid loans, of unrewarded efforts of childrearing and, in general, of giving without having the recipients reciprocate. Thus people seem frequently to live in an atmosphere of frustration and ingratitude and fail to realize that gratitude is mostly the expectation of future favors. We are less inclined to give in compensation for favors received in the past than in the expectation of future favors. Few recognize this. There is a story which has been told of an old gondolier in Venice who refused to sell his gondola although he needed the money for food. He explained his stubbornness by saying that one must always have something to leave.

Not to be able to engage in exchange is the essential tragedy of old age and particularly of the terminally ill person. People have little reason to expect future benefits from them. This can be observed in the last years of a person's career. The closer one gets to retirement, the shorter will be the time that he or she can still do something for the promotion of one's associates, except to create a vacancy by disappearing from the scene. The present of a gold watch at retirement parties may be a cruel symbol of the fact that time is "ticking away" for the recipient, and show that he has no more gold to give.

It has been the practice among the peasants of Europe to give up the management of the farm and sometimes also title to it to one of their grownup sons; they make arrangements for their own support by stipulating the right to keep a cow or two in the pasture, to keep a number of chickens, and to get a number of quarts of milk per week as well as some flour and other victuals from the son to whom they have given the farm. It has been common experience that these forms of support have been grudgingly given. This has frequently been considered to be meanness and ingratitude, but in reality it frequently is a recognition that no more can be expected from the parents. They have turned from potential givers into recipients.

In modern times and urban conditions, the financial support of parents has shifted from being a filial duty to being an obligation of the government. Social security, old age assistance, and private pensions, as well as interest from savings, have taken the place of filial support. This, however, is usually sufficient only until failing health requires institutionalization. Here middle class people frequently engage in inordinate expenditures to secure bodily care and protection for aged persons which they are, or which they feel unable to give themselves. Needles to say, such financial burdens are usually assumed with the expectation that the end is in sight. Again, one could call this heartless, hostile, or the expression of a death wish. The reality, however, is that a regressed parent requiring institutionalization in a convalescent home is unlikely to give anything in return for the financial burden that he or she puts upon the grownup and aging sons and daughters. In some cases old people live on and on, and instead of leaving their sons and daughters an inheritance, they leave them with debts to pay. The tragedy of aging lies, therefore, in the gradual disappearance from the web of reciprocity.

Not only do one's own capacities for reciprocity diminish; so do those of friends in one's age group. They may move to retirement communities or old age homes; they may become too tired to meet with their friends in the evening; they may get sick, and some of them may die.

In relation to younger people, even where reciprocity exists, friendship in the sense of a shared life cannot be experienced between the old and young. Because young people do not know the conditions under which their elders grew up and developed mentally, the old remain strangers to them. On the other hand, though old people have the opportunity to know the conditions under which young people have grown up, they may not approve of or understand the results. In times of rapid social change this lack of sympathy is probably one of the greatest problems of relationships between adult sons and daughters and their aging parents.

In a materialistic world the old are unlikely partners for profitable exchanges. This situation is aggravated by the fact that old people, in their awareness of declining physical and financial powers, are likely to become angry, hostile and spiteful, instead of behaving so that their younger associates do not have to become afraid of them. They consciously or unconsciously stimulate the anxieties of others regarding their own advancing years. The remark, "When you are as old as I am, you will see what it means to be old," is the best means for creating one's own solitude.

It can often be observed in apartment houses especially built for old people, and in homes for the aged, how reluctantly sons and daughters, themselves advancing in years, come to visit their aging parents. One gains the impression that they have to brace themselves to tolerate being targets for hostility without expressing their own hostility in turn. Many are uncertain whether they will pass the test, and many fail.

There are other factors in the mounting anger of aged people and their associations with one another. The deafness of an old person requires other people to talk louder than they would otherwise, to repeat what they have said, and sometimes to feel that they do not get their meaning across. Older people become irritated, not only by their own failing, but also by the signals of irritation which they receive from the people who try to communicate with them. "Raising one's voice" is not seen as an expression of love, but one of anger. The many exchanges of aged with younger people, particularly relatives, seem, therefore, like exchanges of hostility rather than exchanges of love.

Another source of irritation is forgetfulness. Older people forget their immediate past, repeat questions that have just been answered, repeat statements they have just made, and exasperate people by telling well-remembered stories of earlier years over and over again. The old person frequently knows that he or she creates boredom. While it never seems too much for a parent to suffer the repetition of his or her child, it is almost intolerable for a grownup son or daughter to suffer the repetitions of a senile or regressed parent. If one does right by one's parent because ethics demands it, doing the right thing can be its own reward. However, ethics in family life is interfered with by the hostilities which were generated through childhood limitations, through the persistence of parental claims of authority over the sons' and daughters' behavior, and through the offspring's angry reactions to this.

The maternal care of infants is by and large unconditional. It relieves discomforts of the immature child. It cleans and soothes. But as the child matures, parental care changes in character: it begins to set limits and make demands. When the child is able to move itself and objects, to cross streets, and so on, limits must be set on the exercise of these newly-gained abilities. The playpen is the child's first prison. In later stages of maturation, the setting of limits by parents becomes psychological rather than physical. Parents wish to have their children home at certain hours of the night. They object to playmates, boy and girl friends, drug use, and political activities. In essence, they protest the protest of the young. Even after sons and daughters have become adults, parents often do not stop "parenting." In consequence, parent and child relationships contain elements of antagonism and irritation which make interaction difficult and which often cause it to be experienced as non-caring even where care is intended.

When parents grow old, the relationship is reversed. Sons and daughters become caretakers while parents are the receivers of care. The element of hostility becomes aggravated by the role reversal. This is why it is easier for a young nurse, a young aid, or a young companion to listen to the reminiscing, and to bear the forgetfulness of an older person, than it is for the person's children and friends. With her incomparable insight, Simone de Beauvoir cautions us that even the mutual relationships of the aged are "ambiguous": "Old people are like mirrors for one another, mirrors in which they do not care to see themselves."

It would seem therefore that aging, to become tolerable for all concerned, must increasingly become a professional care problem instead of a family care problem. Fee-for-service, together with the desensitization of professional work, make the interaction between the professional and the old person a feasible exchange rather than a mutually unsatisfactory and painful encounter. One must also begin to work on an etiquette of aging which makes behavior in old age subject to certain norms for controlling hostility, which helps to diminish expressions of irritation, and which generally makes the behavior of aged people tolerable to younger persons. The decrease of fertility rates and the effectiveness of medicine in prolonging life has increased the proportion and number of people in their sixties and seventies. This population group should not be left without formulated and agreed-upon norms of behavior which would protect them from driving others away and dooming themselves to die "old and alone."

The declining number of meaningful exchanges in advancing years has led many old people to rely on pseudo-exchanges. Waiting for the mailman to exchange a few words with him or her, waiting for the milkman to do the same, going shopping to engage in conversation with sales personnel — these activities give old people a feeling of manageable and predictable social contact. Letter carriers, premium collectors, and meter readers can be counted upon to become much more reliable in this stage than friends and family members. Even friends are more reliable in this stage of life than family members. It has been observed that widows form what could be called "mutual aid societies." They call one another in the morning to make sure that the other is still all right. They report to one another the events of the previous day. They talk about their illnesses and their contacts with doctors, they arrange to go together to matinees or to luncheons if their finances permit, and interestingly enough, they use the telephone like adolescents, enthusiastically and repetitively. In all their various forms these exchanges may be superficial, but their superficiality makes them emotionally easy. Between sons and daughters on the one hand and parents on the other, and between brothers and sisters, the exchanges are usually emotionally more complex and likely to be experienced as burdens rather than as support.

5

The Challenge of Changing Family Roles

In the preceding chapter we pointed out that non-familial exchanges are less likely to be troubled than exchanges and interactions among family members, and that family relationships are by definition conflict relationships. Parents must exercise discipline, either by corporal or verbal punishment, when the limits which they have set are transgressed. Adolescents are generally rebellious and do not know what their parents want them to do, or disagree with them if they do. Young adults frequently marry people of whom their parents disapprove. They arouse tremendous worry and concern in their parents when they get divorced. They generally resent the attempts of parents to advise them. Parents, in turn, cannot help resenting the amount of trouble, care, service and responsibility which their children represent.

From birth on, parents are told in various ways that they don't understand their children, and they know in their hearts this is true. Children demand attention beyond the power of many parents to give it, and when children fail to develop according to social expectations, the parents are often blamed for having "botched the job." If a child is difficult in school, the school will look to the home as the cause. If children remain unmarried, many people will accuse the parents of not having released them emotionally, thereby making it impossible for them to get married. This reproach continues for all disabilities or "abnormalities." Even more harmful to relationships, many parents love children only at certain ages: some love babies, some love preschoolers, some love adolescents or young adults. Whatever the preferred age of a child from the parents' point of view, the child necessarily grows out of it.

These days, when society is constantly in flux, parents have the additional difficulty of having been socialized in a subculture different from the one in which their children must find their bearings. For people who were adolescents in the depression it is very difficult to understand and accept that their children want to take a year out of school or college to "find themselves." That one has to take a year of apparently doing nothing to decide what occupation or profession one wants to choose, or whether to work against the establishment, is beyond the grasp of many parents who did menial jobs during the daytime and went to school at night to become lawyers or accountants. Mothers who took care of their children at home through teenage years often find it impossible to understand their grownup daughters who drop off their infants in daycare centers while they go off to graduate school or a job. Helena Lopata, perhaps the foremost student of widowhood in the United States, finds that the cultural difference between the generations leads to a "mutual rejection of values and standards, which sometimes results in an outright refusal to have grandparents participate in the socialization of the children." Sons and daughters in adolescence and in early adulthood constantly feel pressure to explain their life and its meaning to their parents. The modern drug culture and the sexual revolution worry even those parents whose children lead relatively traditional lives. They continue to be apprehensive that their children are deceiving them. Similarly, it becomes difficult for sons and daughters in their fifties to explain their lives, its hazards and rewards to their parents in their seventies.

The parent-child relationship is ambivalent by nature: this must affect the relationship when the parents get old and the children have passed the prime of life. Still and all, the parent-child relationship is probably the strongest tie between human beings. Between mother and children it is really biological unity, between father and children it is the strong sociel tie of the namegiver and, in many instances, of the provider.

Most of all, the parent-child relationship is the relationship "one has to have." People without children are in one way or another considered deviant. When a childless person is asked whether he or she has children, one can frequently detect a note of embarrassment when the person has to say "no" to the question. There is an implication of sexual inadequacy, or of imprudence in postponing reproductive sexual activity. What children do for their parents is, therefore, first of all, to document and demonstrate the fertility of the mother and the virility of the father.

It is equally clear that the children, for their self-image, need to have the presence and knowledge of their parents. For a child to be an orphan, adopted, a child of divorce, or an institutionally raised child, suggests that he or she is unloved, singled out by misfortune, and in one way or another not as well off as children who live with their parents. Not to live with both parents requires an explanation and frequently affects warm interactions with others. With all the difficulties on both conscious and unconscious levels, parents and children still need one another; nothing else can take their place. There is, therefore, a true tension between generations: one cannot totally enjoy them, and one cannot be without them.

The old conflicted feelings of love and resentment remains with daughters and sons who have aged parents, but the power and role relationships are reversed. People in their forties do not need to be cared for by parents anymore, and regressed people in their late seventies and their eighties no longer need children but do need caretakers. Adult children may find that the burdens of caring for their aged parents conflict with the financial needs of their adolescent and college-age children. Simultaneously, the adult children may begin to experience the first signs of their own aging: they are more easily fatigued; they have less strength; they begin to see physical signs of aging in their mirrors.

The poor health of aging parents or of the "aging" sons and daughters will interfere with the maintenance of the exchange principle. Still, contacts are likely to be carried on and only rarely dwindle away completely. Apparently, filial duties toward parents have always been difficult. This is suggested by the fact that the fourth commandment of Yahweh to Moses asks sons and daughters to honor their parents. It is interesting to note that this is the only commandment promising human rewards for procreation and long life.

We should also consider here the consequences of divorce and remarriage for intergenerational exchanges. People who have left their spouses and children to live alone or to start a second marriage can rarely expect the sons and daughters of their first marriage to have forgotten the feelings of abandonment and resentment which they have caused. Often such feelings are shared and reinforced by the parent who retains custody. These persons will sometimes incite hatred against the spouse who has left them, making the children partners of his or her own hurt and feelings of injustice.

Remarriage of widowed older persons may also raise the opposition of the children, who may feel that their widowed parent will be exploited when he or she marries a younger person. Even if the second spouse is a partner of similar age, there will be frequently justifiable apprehension about change of wills and the problems of relating to a stranger who has entered the web of family relationships. It is not surprising, then, that alienation between family members should result when a parent remarries.

Of course, as always in human relationships, there are usually benefits where there are disadvantages. Middle-aged sons and daughters may feel relieved of the total burden of interaction when aged parents remarry. Where two social security or pension incomes are joined, there may be relief from the feeling that one has to make financial contributions to the parent.

Still another way of coping with the problems of intergenerational exchange is geographical mobility. In this country, young and old are on the move. Occupational advance for the young and middle-aged is often connected with a move from one city to another. For old persons, a move to warmer climates and residential communities far from where their children live may bring about alienation by distance, or, just as feasibly, it may reduce friction. In some instances a move may be used for just this purpose. This is again an instance of the contradictions which will always be found in patterns of human interactions. Whether such a move is adaptive or not, only experience can tell. It is a principle of problem solution never to repeat or continue what has not worked.

In contrast to the almost invariable conflict experienced between parents and children, the experience between parents and grandchildren seems to be less frequently and less intensely conflicted. Grandchildren represent a further step toward biological immortality. In general the grandchildren do not need the constant care of the grandparents. The grandmothers do not have to be pregnant with them; they do not have to nurse them; the grandfathers are not usually responsible for their upbringing or for providing them with financial support. Grandchildren in the middle and upper classes carry no obligation of childrearing. The grandmother role usually demands no more than babysitting, reading stories, playing games and dropping in to visit. If the grandchildren should turn out badly, it will of course be a sorrow, but it will be the mother or father who will be blamed, and the grandparents themselves may join those blaming the parents. So, while they offer great joy and little responsibility, grandchildren also testify to the fact that one has fulfilled the biblical command to "multiply and replenish the earth."

In some population groups grandmothers still have an obligation to rear grandchildren, particularly when the mother is working. Those people experience the conflicts of parenting exaggerated by social change, because they are two generations removed. Grandparents' role as childrearers seems to be diminishing, however, as a result of the tremendous impact of institutional child care, new thinking about what children experience in their early years, and permissiveness in the children's worlds of daycare centers, nursery schools, and kindergartens. This change in values in modern childrearing probably pervades all classes and tends to weaken the link between grandparents and grandchildren.

Difficulties between adult children and their parents may arise from irresponsible exchange with the grandchildren. Grandparents, because they are not obligated to exercise limiting care, may spoil the grandchildren. There is less risk of irritating consequences, because in many families, particularly in the middle class, grandparents do not live in the parental household of the children. Visits are easily borne when compared with living together.

If the life span of people in our society increases, one might visualize a future in which the family care of old people would be entrusted to their grandchildren, rather than to their grownup children. If this ever came about, it would at least produce a relationship which would rarely be under the shadow of past antagonism and irritation, and which would be free from the shadow of mother-in-law relationships. This notion has been dramatized very clearly in the movie "Peage," in which a son cannot comfortably visit his institutionalized mother with his wife. The wife not only resents the spectre of decay for herself, but also resents the visit because it means renewed contact with "the mother-in-law." The son is uncomfortable and sad, still torn between two women. But one of the grandsons engages the grandmother in a meaningful relationship. He helps her to reminisce about the pleasant times she had with him, and he with her, and so salvages the family's visit to the institution. It is important to point out that he could easily perform this service because his grandmother gave him only good times; after all, she did not have to bring him up. Therefore, one could almost say that the only potential for satisfactory intergenerational exchanges in the family lies in jumping over one generation.

6

Adapting Homes to Advancing Years

We are born and die in hospitals. From the maternity ward, we are brought to the home of our parents, or in cases of abandonment in hospital, to an institution. In the home of our parents we are sheltered, nurtured, and cared for. As maturation proceeds, however, we are limited in the use of space. We may not enter the bedroom of our parents when they wish privacy; we may not enter a bathroom when the door is closed. We may not bang on the furniture or use crayons on the walls. We may even be excluded from the use of the rest of the house or apartment by being sent to our room as punishment, making our room a place of confinement rather than a shelter. All this has been referred to as limiting care, and the parental home is an arena for the battles that this care implies.

The parental home is, therefore, a shelter without autonomy. It is not our home, but our parents' home. Frequently we must share it with siblings who annoy us and mess up our things. It may be a place where we have to do maintenance work, such as cleaning, taking out trash, and keeping our room in order. We do this work not because we feel that it is necessary, but because our parents ask us to do it. In many instances we must return to it at an hour specified by our parents. If we break this "curfew" we may be disciplined with even greater strictness.

Usually with maturation American children separate increasingly from the home of their parents. A part of the day is spent in childcare institutions, schools, or summer camps, which may well be either an exile from the home, or a liberation from the prison that the home represents. College dormitories also bring liberation from the parental home, though like all strange environments, they also bring into perspective the benefits, warmth, security, and feeling of belonging which the parental home provides. This primary experience of the parental home stays with us until either the home or the parents disappear.

With the independence of young adulthood comes the experience of one's own home. Perhaps finances make sharing an apartment necessary. At any rate, one's roommate, congenial or not, does not have parental authority in our home. He or she may be an irritant, but the irritation can be removed by finding a more congenial partner or by eventually deciding to live alone. Whether one finally decides on marriage or singlehood as a lifestyle, one's residence finally becomes one's "own" home.

In the case of marriage the irritations of living with another person may be as great as those experienced by living in the home of a parent or with a roommate, yet the new feeling is one of ownership and territoriality. One now has the power to exclude and becomes master of a spot in space. Normally, this power of territoriality must still be shared with a spouse, but it is a new and significant experience. This autonomy over one's home is in jeopardy in old age. The loss threatens old people, who must move in with relatives or enter an institution such as so-called convalescent homes. Even those people who, after a child has left, decide to move to a smaller house, condominium, or an apartment are likely to suffer a feeling of diminished territoriality which is part of the loss experienced in old age. A recent experiment called "Operation Match" which is designed to pair older home owners desiring services with people who want a place to live, either as a barter arrangement or on a straight rental basis, may be the best solution for people in advanced years who do not want to move.

In describing the psychological and sociological meaning of one's own home, one is tempted to compare it with the skin of one's body. It is, of course, a wider skin, and the skin is not organic but composed of brick and mortar, but it is nevertheless a boundary defining, limiting, and protecting one's existence in the world. It is a place where one has control, even if it be shared with a spouse, instead of being a place where one is controlled.

In old age people frequently cling to their homes because they dread the shift from being in charge to not being in charge. Having come into the world helpless, and having grown through years and years of being controlled by parents or childrearers, we view our own home symbolically; we connect it with the best years of our lives, the years in which we are "on top," so to speak, and do not have to take or defy orders. The old person senses that upon leaving this home he or she will have to take orders again. To give up one's own home in a very real sense may mean to return to the limitations of childhood.

There are other meanings attached to one's marital home. It is a place where the sexual union between the spouses usually takes place. The home represents not only moments of sexual felicity, but in a wider sense, the completeness which a person living alone cannot experience. It is probably one of the strongest components of loss for the surviving spouse that the feeling of completeness is gone. This loss is also felt by the associates of the survivor who were accustomed to think of him or her as part of a couple. When the unity is destroyed, the survivor and his or her associates must begin to think of the person as a "single," a fraction which now must become a total entity again. According to Jung, facing separation is the greatest and the hardest task of being human, and nowhere will one be so reminded of this task as in the home after a spouse has died.

Actually separation occurs earlier in many cases, when the children leave home to set up independent living. The feeling of the "empty nest" is a feeling of separation and loss. But it is mitigated by the fact that it is not produced by death and may lead to the procreation of grandchildren and more people in the "life space" of the parents. With the departure of the children, people may have to face the fact that their home has become too large for them. They may experience the burden and discomforts of such shelter, its emptiness and possible neglect, its demand for outside help which is not available. Yet they may still fight the idea of leaving it. Occasionally one reads of old people being found dead in their homes where they have spent their last days unattended and unnoticed. Like the gondolier, they may have wanted something to leave.

Some older people, however, do not feel up to managing the family home, and they move to a smaller house or apartment. This brings about significant experiences of being diminished. However, the adaptation through change to a more manageable and appropriate living space, though painful, may be a victory of realism, a proof that one is able to adapt. There may be fewer rooms, but cleaning and paying for them will be easier, with lower rent, taxes, and maintenance costs. There may also be other advantages resulting from this change. One may choose any residential area now, not just one determined by nearness to a school or job; one may have no more lawns to cut, plumbing or electric wiring to repair and, possibly, no more real estate taxes to pay. The shelter may not demand from you more than you can afford in money or give to it in attention. Still, like all changes, it asks its price: one's social skin, one's shelter, has become smaller.

In the case of the death of a spouse, adaptation to smaller living space may not only be a necessity from the viewpoint of management. It may also give the survivor the feeling of a home with unshared autonomy. Whereas one may have yielded to the ideas of the other on interior decorations, on mealtimes, on bedtimes, on whom to invite, and whom not to invite to visit, now the survivor will truly be "master" in the house. He or she may be burdened with bereavement, sorrow, and apprehension regarding his or her own death. But still, being master of one's own life-space is a new and beneficial experience which probably helps many widows and widowers to regain their strength under the blows of fate.

It is questionable whether one should retain one's shelter after the death of one's spouse. Many reminders of his or her existence will be there; an empty twin bed or an empty space in a shared bed in the bedroom must be a daily reminder that he or she slept there. This can heighten anxiety for oneself. The absence represents a coffin in the survivor's life.

Rearrangement of furniture may affirm one's autonomy and correct the concessions that one has made to the taste of another. If one moves to a smaller home, it is important to maintain a number of material comforts, objects which have almost become a part of oneself, extensions of one's ego. "My chair," no matter how much space it takes in a much smaller house, should be there. One's favorite china or silver should be on display. One's favorite books should be on the shelves, the favorite flower pot on the windowsill. If possible, the new place, though smaller, should be more beautiful or satisfying than the old one, have a better view, be closer to public transportation, churches, public libraries, and shops.

For the aging person who has chosen the single lifestyle, some of these adaptations in the home may not be necessary. A declining capacity for work one has formerly done effortlessly will, however, require similar changes. Yard work may become unmanageable, housework too hard, and friends may move away, producing loneliness where formerly there was a tightly knit web of neighbors. The adaptation of a single person to a smaller life-space may be easier because it will not include or follow the loss of a spouse.

At this stage in life one must apply ingenuity in making work easier for oneself, or find people who will do work which one formerly did oneself. For example, the senior author, when bending became too hard for him, discovered that he could take an aluminum chair and push it along the borders of his garden when he needed to weed and trim. He could do a better job this way because it was less painful. Of course, a sitting gardener, pushing his chair from spot to spot, is an unusual picture, but he had adapted and found a method which worked.

An important point in doing housework or yard work in advancing years is the increasing risk of accidents and the lower chance of recovery. Compared with these risks, services, even if one has to pay for them, will turn out to be bargains. High school and college students are frequently available to work at reasonable prices.

Of course, living alone in old age implies loneliness and anxiety about being unattended when one has an accident in the home or gets sick. There is also the fear of burglars, part of the general apprehension of old people that they will be victimized by crime at home and in the streets. For this reason also, many old people have arranged monitoring services, or regular telephone calls with friends, in order to find out whether the other is all right. As a byproduct, such calls also relieve loneliness for both parties. Such monitoring services are also available commercially, but they cannot provide the quality of the half-hour conversation that such a call among friends does or can do.

Many old people choose to move to retirement villages, such as Sun City in Arizona, Leisureworld in Southern California or smaller places such as Dunwoody or Kendall in Pennsylvania. Certainly these communities make life easier. Lawns are kept, repairs are provided, and infirmary service is available for those for whom independent living has become impossible. People with means and strong dependency needs, or health conditions which require another climate, will find moving to such places a satisfactory way to adapt to the physical and social changes of their life. From a social point of view one must ask, however, whether these are not in fact places of self-chosen segregation, and whether they will not be experienced — at least by some — as diminishing in an unintended way. One must also remember that in these places mortality rates are high and that living in a place where people are likely to die is a constant reminder of death. This cannot help but raise the death anxieties of other members of the community. Similar considerations apply to apartment houses for the elderly which have become common in our society, and of which York House in Philadelphia and Isabella House in New York are examples. Here again, a measure of independence is prescribed, housekeeping services are provided, meals are available, and lunch and dinner sometimes are mandatory. However, the segregation problems and mortality problems remain. Infirmaries for helpless or regressed people are attached to these places, and by their very proximity they may raise thoughts of the impending end. One might be tempted to say that one must either believe in a life after death or be a very dependent person to prefer these arrangements to facing death in a home of one's own. People who believe in a life after death, of course, may find in old age communities maintained by religious orders a spiritual rapport which is life-enhancing, if not life-sustaining. Psalm 71 beautifully expresses this rapport:

> Now that I am old and gray,
> God, do not desert me . . .
> You have done great things;
> Who, God, is comparable to you?
> You have sent me misery and hardship,
> but you will give me life again,
> You will pull me up again from the depths
>   of the earth,
> Prolong my old age, and once more comfort
>   me.

Psalm 71: 18-22 (The Jerusalem Bible)

Ultimately, of course, physical infirmities, mental deterioration, pressure by relatives, or terminal disease may force old people into institutional care. Such institutions, last stops before the cemetery, are frequently places of sedation where people move toward death without being fully aware of the process. However, under modern conditions there may be no alternatives. Old people may endanger themselves or others if not institutionalized. They may cause fires, develop ideas of persecution, or become, by their presence, disturbers of the peace in their sons' or daughters' family lives. Naturally, children may feel guilty when they place their parents in institutional care, but it is sometimes the best option.

Institutional life for substantial numbers of people, be they children or adults, emotionally disturbed or physically handicapped, requires rules of management which diminish the patients' life choices. Hannah Arendt's three "human conditions" — labor, productivity, and the blessing of the active life — are taken away from them. It becomes a vegetable existence, disturbed by fear of death, fear of being mistreated by aides, fear of using up one's resources, fear of being a burden to sons and daughters who often find it difficult to carry the financial responsibility of maintaining an old parent in such homes. If such life continues and does not lead to oblique suicide, we must conclude that there is still a primary wish to live, which, although meaningless to others, must have meaning to the self, perhaps no more than a drowsy feeling of hanging-on to the ultimate value of life.

When one member of a couple is forced into a severely reduced form of existence, the suffering of the spouse may be equal if not greater. To see a beloved one deteriorate into terminality not only raises one's own death anxieties but also arouses feelings of guilt if one has placed such a person in a "dying station." Arnold Toynbee and others have made the important point that there are always two parties to dying, the person who dies and the survivors.

7

Loss: Loneliness and Liberation

The word "loss" has a connotation of misfortune, of sorrow, of failure, of being diminished. It is a negative in life. Yet it seems that human beings have a remarkable capacity to live on bravely and often successfully after loss has occurred. If it were not so, one might wonder how people manage to lose their youth, their vitality, their jobs, their friends, their spouses and sometimes their children without being driven to despair.

This apparent enigma can be solved if one realizes that the loss of a person or object is frequently followed by substitution, which one could not have enjoyed if the loss had not occurred. The loss of youth sets one free for maturity, the loss of childhood and adolescence for adulthood, the loss of a lover for another love. The departure of children sets one free from the demands and roles of child care. Even the loss of a spouse may set one free for another spouse. In essence, then, losses are liberators. The dynamics of living and development require such compensations as a reason to go on. A famous psychiatrist, John Bowlby, identified the three stages of mourning as: an urge to recover the lost object, disorganization, and subsequent reorganization.

The suffering caused by loss of friends, relatives, spouses, or parents is, of course, the renewal of loneliness. Since human beings need other human beings for exchanges, the loss of an associate to whom one has become attached in a long series of exchanges is likely to leave one bereaved, depressed, and essentially fearful. One feels unattended and does not quite see who will take the lost person's place.

It also takes time to build up new intimacies. Without knowing at least part of another's history, reactions, and specific vulnerabilities, one cannot become intimate in friendships, love, or marriage. Particularly in the latter, one must also learn to relate to the persons of significance in the spouse's life. Mothers- and fathers-in-law, brother- and sisters-in-law, and friends cannot be ignored. One enters their family system and has to try to become part of it. In other words, becoming close to one person cannot be done quickly and without involvement with other people. All this requires a length of time which old people are unlikely to have. They are, therefore, at a disadvantage in making substitutions for losses they have suffered. Also one may feel guilty over wrongs that one may have done to the departed, or for death wishes which one may have had in cases of prolonged terminality. To overcome such feelings of remorse is hard psychological labor. One may simply feel disloyal to the departed by replacing him or her with another person. Social mores, however, permit a compromise between the feeling of loyalty and the need for substitution. There are time-limited periods of mourning which people are supposed to observe. After the expiration of these periods, one is free to look for substitutions, to drop the mask of sadness and to go on living.

In another sense the loss is not only a liberator from the constraints created by earlier ties, but it may also give one a chance for better experiences. A lost friend may set you free for a better friend, a divorce for a better spouse and, in the material realm, the loss of a job may set you free for a better job. People become prisoners of their success if such an experience forces them to continue on a road which, on consideration, they might have preferred not to travel. For example, administrators in the church, in government, in education and in business find that the exercise of power leads to negative criticism which they did not foresee. In retrospect many people who have not attained their professional goals will find that they have been spared much heart-ache and public censure by what seemed to be a loss at the time. Those who get ahead through promotions and attain higher income and status may subsequently find themselves caught doing work they really do not want to do. They may miss a feeling of authenticity in their work.

Similar situations exist in marriage. A couple may feel they do not love each other any more, but if there are children they may feel obligated to give them a home and an upbringing. By the time the children grow up, one may feel loyalty regardless of lack of love and hesitate to leave the spouse at that stage. And so the "law of good continuation" may lead to a life of silent despair. For such people, loss or failure is the only thing that will set them free to pursue new goals.

It is true, of course, that life runs on a narrowing track and that alternatives become fewer and harder to obtain as one passes the middle of life. One is "over the hill" and becomes less desirable to others. One has also less of a future to offer to others, and it is a future with the prospect of increasing deterioration. So it is likely that people in advanced years will have difficulty in finding appropriate substitutes for friends, spouses, jobs, and even hobbies or sports for which they have lost the necessary capacity.

This diminishing of the life-space, however, goes hand in hand with diminishing vitality and so establishes a new balance. In organic life, disturbance always is followed by a rearrangement of forces which one calls "homeostasis," a tendency toward order and stability. A similar phenomenon exists in social life. Time set free is filled by new pursuits. If one is retired, one may find that the maintenance of the home takes the hours that were formerly spent at the office. If one has lunch with a friend one may need the afternoon to rest up.

In the realm of human relationships there is always ambivalence. Any object may elicit opposite feelings, especially love and hate. The experience of ambivalence is probably felt most strongly in family life and social relations. Nobody is perfect. No spouse, no child, no brother or sister, no friend has all the qualities which we wish they had, and all of them have qualities which we wish they did not have. It is difficult, therefore, to imagine a spouse, relative, or friend who has not on occasion created hostility, impatience, annoyance, or boredom in us.

Successful and originally satisfying careers eventually become routine or give one the feeling of obsolescence or of being surrounded by impatient successors. One may not want to retire because of the structure that a job gives to one's life, the prestige attached to one's position, and the income which such an employment provides, but one will become ambivalent about continuing — and about retiring.

Retirement ceremonies, memorial services, and funerals may conceal the reality that the person who is being lost to his or her associates was difficult to bear. It is not acceptable to acknowledge ambivalence about a loss. This social constraint is likely to misrepresent the experience of loss. We are exhorted to say nothing but good about the dead and to feel nothing but love or friendship for the departed. Yet the very limitations of mourning periods in all cultures and the feeling "that life must go on" suggest that feelings, in reality, are always mixed. If this were not so, it would be difficult to understand how so many widows go on without their husbands. The death of a spouse in a bad marriage or from a painful, terminal disease, must give the survivor a feeling of relief even if mixed with the feeling of guilt. The death of a friend with whom contact has become routine may be the end of dutifully tolerated boredom. Even the loss of possessions may free one from worry, from responsibility, from problems of maintenance, from the cost of repairs and from being grounded in space as well as in time. The person who no longer goes to business saves on both clothes and commuting expenses.

To come to another experience of loss in advancing years, let us explore the "comforts" of deafness. Deafness produces serious disorders in communication and social organization. It requires new adaptive skills, such as tolerance for hearing aid use or lip reading. It is a standing joke that deaf people carry their hearing aids in their pockets; it cannot easily be grasped by critics that deafness provides a measure of peace which must be experienced to be appreciated. A world of silence is a world of peacefulness. Sounds neither attract nor distract. One can concentrate on what one is doing.

Even blindness has some minimal compensation. At night, instead of lying awake, disturbed by the light from the window, a visually impaired person can sleep, oblivious to stimuli from outside, stimuli which force one to respond. Walking along strings put up in one's yard, taking a walk along a familiar path alone, and even walking with a Seeing Eye dog are achievements which give the feeling of conquering one of the most serious handicaps that can befall a human being.

The beginning stages of deafness and blindness protect those afflicted against invasion by stimuli to which they might be too weak or too tired to respond. And apart from the physiological and concomitant psychological feelings of temporary well-being, coping with both the onset and development of these impairments represents a challenge of adaptation which may lead to victories of the ego and resulting satisfaction.

The senior author must draw on his own experiences with a hearing difficulty. Being a professor accustomed to considerable use of classroom discussion, he started to concentrate more on what was said in the classroom than on what was said in the outside world. He developed two levels of hearing, one for his students and one for others. When the impairment increased, he explained his condition in class and asked his students to give him visible signs that they wanted to say something. If such a sign came, he left his chair and walked toward the student until he reached hearing distance and started the discussion. Still later, when surgery had weakened him, he asked students to come nearer for a restatement of what had been said. He put an empty chair next to his own and invited students to come and sit with him if they wanted to open up a discussion.

Marital life implies accommodation to another person's demands and standards. As there are compensations in other areas of loss, so there are also physical benefits that may come with the loss of a marriage partner. To be able to eat when one wants, and what one wants, to be able to read at night without having to wake up a spouse, or without having to lie sleepless in order to protect the sleep of the other, are experiences of compensation which are important to recognize in understanding how people overcome losses. The survivor will be able to follow his or her standard of living rather than adjust to the living standard preferred by the other. Life insurance and inheritance may give the survivor the experience of being financially better off than before, though with current rates of inflation this may become unlikely. At any rate, financial adaptations, upward or downward, will be unobstructed by the expectations and preferences of the departed.

Viktor E. Frankl, author of *Man's Search For Meaning,* once said that the greatest comfort of a survivor is to have the thought that the departed has been spared survivorship. A strong tabu frequently prevents people from thinking out their wishes in this respect. Do they want to go first and leave their partners the loneliness and difficulties of coping with a life that has always been handled as a team? Does a husband want to see his wife suddenly faced with mail which she never read, with decisions about investments which she never had to make, with deciding whether to change her home to more appropriate space and expense? Does he want her to start thinking about a successor to him? Similarly, does the wife want her husband to cope with problems of household management which he always left to her, to take care of his own meals, to sit alone in the living room which he has shared with her for decades? Does she want him in his fantasies to run after young women who will either scorn him or exploit him? Does she want to see him deprived of that maternal care which (at least for people who have attained old age in the Seventies) is a frequent experience which almost all husband-wife relationships imply and without which he would be somewhat lost? Although he or she might have been irritated with the previous division of labor, no matter what its nature, the survivor now must cope with additional responsibilities.

It is likely that most people try not to face these questions and are willing to let things arrange themselves. Much of this arranging usually falls to women. There are more widows than widowers, and it can be observed that women seem to be able to cope with being survivors better than men. The fact that widowers often die soon after their wives' deaths suggests another phenomenon: just as without nurture infants will stop thriving and die in spite of sanitation and food that an institution may provide, so the continuity of the maternal stance which women use in interaction with their husbands contains an element of nurture without which men cannot live long.

The problem of widowhood is probably not so much the actual experience of the condition over time, as it is the trauma of the transition. To be a widow is relatively easy. To become one is hell. There is first of all the shock of sudden death. To learn that one's husband has collapsed in the office and has been found "dead on arrival" at the hospital is something which one probably cannot at first believe or fully grasp. To find one's wife dead next to oneself in the morning represents the same mixture of the incredible and the horrible. Here the trauma is sudden, met without preparation and undoubtedly with great suffering. Still, the shock may mean that recovery takes less time.

The trauma of widowhood, however, may have begun long before the death of the spouse. Then there is not only anticipatory grief and the burden of taking care of an increasingly demanding and increasingly hopeless situation; there is also the uncertainty and the apprehension over one's own ability to handle life alone which one has always handled with another. This is a period of crisis: one doesn't know how one will cope; one is anxious; and the fact that innumerable other people have handled similar situations holds no comfort. At this period the terminal person has to hold the hand of the nonterminal person. As in every crisis, there is no place for argument, no mood is illegitimate. Only time can be the healer, but until time has done its job, the dying spouse or other close associates can do nothing but "be there." One can lend to the anticipatory mourner nothing more than an affirmative presence which even the dying have it still in their power to give. One can listen to the expressions of anticipatory grief and not contest the mood. By being a comforter, one demonstrates that he or she is not a corpse.

Of course the dying have their own anxieties. The dying spouse may somehow send a signal that he or she — legitimately — has personal worries. What this period ultimately amounts to is surviving from hour to hour, from day to day, from month to month.

After that dying period has been lived through, there comes a time in which it makes a great difference whether the widow or widower has a meaningful role other than housework, such as a profession, a civic responsibility, or organizational functions, such as Board memberships or volunteer work. These roles are ego-maintaining and, more important, they can be expanded to fill the gap created by the loss of a spouse. For a woman, housework, however bravely continued, does not seem to have the same ego-supporting quality.

Only when the losses make one completely helpless and no substitutes can be found will the loss stop being a liberator and become a threat to life. This is particularly true when losses follow in quick succession. When people approach the seventies they are likely to be reminded of their mortality by repetitive news of terminal diseases and death among their friends and relatives. As one grows older it becomes more and more difficult to find substitutes for friends and spouses because one's image of these persons is always one of young people. It is very difficult to become friends with a person who has not known one in some active context. These are strangers. Why would they care?

Most people think of a marriage partner, a companion, or even a date as a young person. The fantasy of many an old man — and statistics bear this out to a degree — is to marry a young woman. Those, however, who realize that this is for them a hopeless wish begin to develop a self-image which approximates the appearance which they present to others. One of the main losses that leads to depression in old age is probably the realization that one is not eligible for the substitutes of one's own wishing.

As the years roll by, physical decline becomes pervasive. To the losses of hearing and eyesight are added loss of continence, probably one of the hardest insults to one's self-respect, the loss of mobility through arthritis which may have the consequence that one cannot undergo an operation, and ultimately, the loss of the will to live.

In summary, advanced aging contains two kinds of losses: one physical, accompanied by pain, hopelessness of recovery; and the other, the will to continue organic and psychological existence under such conditions. These two losses, however, will be the final liberators from the burden of a life that has become intolerable.

8

The Fantasy of a Second Career

Until 1979, compulsory retirement at age 60 to 65 has been almost universal for employed people and has left many retired people stranded without the status connected with their occupation or profession, with reduced income and with the anxiety-creating problem of unstructured time. Very likely, this experience has been accompanied by a feeling of injustice. Compulsory retirement has frequently been accused of forcing people out of their life's work before their abilities to perform adequately have become impaired. This is undoubtedly true, but the alternative would, in many instances, be much harder to bear. To be retired for age-connected inadequacies would surely be much more hurtful than having to retire at a specific age without exception, for the latter has no implications of negative evaluation. This is an advantage of mandatory retirement which frequently remains unrecognized.

Aging, with its increasingly diminishing capacities, makes old people angry with themselves and, by projection, with others. This age-connected hostility is rationalized by focusing on the "injustice" of being treated, not as an individual, but as a member of a category without consideration for individual capacities or merit. Such rationalization may help people to deny their decline of memory, or other old-age impairments, and lead them to contest retirement for such reasons as age discrimination. The fear of such law suits may induce employers to terminate employment before the age question can be raised. On the other hand, the social cost of impartiality is the indisputable fact that substantial numbers of persons must retire while they still feel able to continue, and while they want to work.

Just because of this widespread feeling, and because of the absence of negative implications, many people who are retired are led to think about second careers. However, their plans frequently border on fantasy. Fantasies connected with second career plans are first of all due to the fact that people who have worked throughout most of their adult lives have accumulated considerable dissatisfaction with the work they have done. They have suffered many wounds to their egos in not getting all the rewards to which they have aspired. Many feel they might have escaped boredom, or the disappointment that they have suffered in their careers, if they had only chosen another line of work. The second career is, therefore, a plan which is supposed to provide not only maintenance, and an increase in income, but also the feeling of greater authenticity in work and, hopefully, greater success. It is not only a plan for coping with the present and the future but also a necessarily futile attempt to make up for the disappointments of the past.

Again we see the strong connection between time and hope. Even with obviously diminished time left, people continue to hope and expect from time what in most instances it cannot give. This is in the last analysis the absurdity of existentialism when applied to planning in old age. To connect time and hope is appropriate for young people, but it becomes questionable for the middle-aged of average capacity, and it becomes a neglect of natural law for the aged. To cultivate what one has acquired, and to maintain what one possesses, is a burden difficult enough to carry and, ultimately, may become impossible to carry to the end of life. For this reason Stoicism and Hedonism are better guides than Existentialism for the aged. Existentialism is likely to lead old people astray because it connects hope with insufficient time.

Actually, it is not only the retired who plan a second career. Consideration of other population groups with second career problems may help to clarify the plight of the aged in this respect. Second careers are also the problem of many women whose children have gone to school and who find themselves stranded in relatively early middle age with the essence of the maternal role gone or taken over by the school system. Such women have the feeling that they have still enough time for self-realization and for a shift from a child-oriented to a self-oriented life. The Women's Movement has undoubtedly intensified or even created the need of many such women to think in terms of a second career.

This is a younger population than the retired. Its members usually have time enough to return to school and engage in continuing education, or in refreshing and bringing up to date occupational skills or professional qualifications which they had acquired before becoming absorbed in child care and child rearing. This is an important contrast with the retired, because the retired do not have such time for educational investments. Even if they do go into continuing education, they will probably spend a good part of their remaining years, and a good deal of their remaining strength preparing for something which they would have little time to use. They will be close to their seventies before attaining full professional status.

A third group of second career planners and second career performers is composed of the retired members of the armed forces. Since one can retire after twenty years of service with full pension, and since officers must retire if they have been twice passed over for promotion, they also are people with time for continuing education or preparation for new careers. In many instances, they are welcomed for employment in business and industry because they have gained administrative experience and skills that can quickly be transferred. They are, therefore, the most successful group of second career people in our society.

A fourth and last group of second career planners are people who are sufficiently oriented to existentialism to give up careers which would still have a considerable future, in order to explore other areas of their potential. It is frequently part of the professional expectation of the middle class that jobs should be fun and, if not fun, at least interesting and, if not interesting, at least not disappointing. Since most people in our society must earn their living, almost all of these expectations are likely to remain unfulfilled. Most jobs are not fun; most professional work loses creativity; most experiences of employees are overshadowed by supervision, negative evaluations, and denied promotions. All are in the grip of routinization. This leads existentialists to a feeling of discomfort which demands career change. They do not feel that their work provides authenticity, and so they explore new areas in this search.

Such career changes sometimes border on the absurd. A surgeon becomes a lobsterman, a lawyer opens a restaurant, a manager of a laundry becomes a family therapist, a family therapist becomes a farmer. Such people may enjoy the thrill of change, but they impress many of their friends and former colleagues as persons who have turned away from their exercise of acquired competence to somewhat questionable ventures more becoming to an adolescent that to a mature person.

In the spectrum of such second careers the experience of a person who starts after he or she has reached mandatory retirement age is likely to be the least successful and potentially the most pathetic. Allusion has been made to the important factor of remaining time. Careers require time for preparation, time for practical experience and time to repair one's mistakes. In all of this, the old person is more disadvantaged than any of the other population groups mentioned so far. A professional person such as an engineer may be used by the competition as a consultant for a few years until his or her know-how has become obsolete or has become incorporated into the system of the new employer. A retired college professor may be invited as a visiting professor by another institution for a year or two. But these are only continuations of what one has done, rather than new careers.

Given the human condition and its unpredictability, people cannot avoid being disappointed and making mistakes. They cope with the consequences by promises to do better in the future. Here old people again are at a disadvantage. They may not have enough time left to make up and gain forgiveness for their errors. Frequently they may lack credibility for their promises and fail to get public response.

Where new preparation is required, one must frequently study together with students who could be one's sons and granddaughters. Finding out that young people are not encumbered by old learning and are faster in acquiring new knowledge and skills, and more successful in taking tests may deeply wound the self-image of older people. Not only will the fellow students be younger; so will the teachers. Many people who before retirement have enjoyed established props of seniority will find the status reversal hard to take. They may also feel a frequent lack of motivation. Winston Churchill is quoted as saying that "age takes the wish to learn away from us. It is hard to find new interests at the end of one's life."

Besides the time factor, there is also an unwillingness in people to retype someone in a new role. People refuse to believe in the business acumen of a college professor, or the ability of an accountant to write fiction, or the competence of a nurse or a social worker to run a boutique. We must also emphasize that many of these second career dreams are dreams of self-employment or ownership of small businesses which, almost by definition, cannot compete in our economy of large corporations, department stores, and chains of stores or restaurants. The idea of a franchise may seem to be feasible in such instances, but it consumes capital and turns what should have been a cushion for security into risky speculation. Furthermore, it is emotionally difficult for old people to avoid conservatism in investment and it is probably wise to be conservative at that stage in life. One must also consider that at this stage in life vitality goes down, and illness may interfere with the pursuit of a new career.

Probably all second careers represent fantasies and will suffer from confrontation with reality. Certainly, second careers are under the shadow of shortened time. As pointed out above, second careers frequently require shifting from the role of practicing competence to the role of acquiring competence. The graduate "may have to become a student again." Of course, differences in degree and differences in remaining time must be recognized. One would certainly wish to encourage a woman of 35 or a lieutenant colonel who was retired at 40 to look for a second career, but one would probably be encouraging failure if one counseled an old person to seek a career requiring a whole set of new skills. In order to protect old people against this risk, RSVP, a service established to find retirees activities in which they can retain — or regain — a feeling of fruitful and needed activity, tries to place them in settings in which they can utilize formerly acquired skills.

The problems which old people face are problems of maintenance, of competence, and the harvesting of skills that they have acquired. The scholar may continue to write books in his or her field; the manual worker may enjoy the role of a self-employed jack-of-all-trades; the business executive may become a consultant; the retired nurse may become a companion; the police officer, a security guard; the retired teacher, a tutor; the retired secretary, a free-lance typist.

We live in a society which lends credibility to the young but not to the old. If one continues as far as possible in the line of one's established competence, one may still encounter decreased credibility — or decreased desirability — but one will be at an advantage over those in a totally new field. Many people are cruel to the old, and starting a second career sets one up as a target. Therefore, as a fortress against the cruelty of young people or envious peers, the cultivation of one's acquired competence is still the best bet. This applies to cooking as well as to the study of Scriptures.

9

Remarriage in Old Age

Ninety-five percent of marriages by people in advanced years are remarriages. The word "remarriage," however, indicates intent rather than reality. Old age marriages are all too frequently attempts at restitution of a loss, rather than new ventures. The marriage which one has lost through death of a spouse can never be reconstituted or even approximated through marriage with another person. The marriage with that new person will be another marriage. Thus one cannot really re-marry after the death of a spouse; one can only marry a second time.

Because older women tend to die later than old men, they have a significantly smaller pool of age-appropriate partners available for another marriage. Their opportunities for remarriage are further diminished because old men prefer younger women as new spouses, and they tend to select them from the social set to which they belonged with their former wives. Such attempts at continuity may often fail, because they are based on the public presence of the second spouse. Having gone to concerts together, having invited one another for meals, having been card partners, does not produce the knowledge which intimacy will create. Such knowledge will have to be acquired in the minutiae of daily living, and the second spouse will be found to be different from the first, no matter how much similarity one has perceived. The adjustments made to the former partner are, therefore, unlikely to work with the new. The situation will be made more difficult, because irritations with the former spouse will have disappeared and the past will be gilded, while irritations caused by the new spouse will have to be coped with. Actually no remarriage can be a continuation or a resumption of an earlier marriage. It is unavoidably a new marriage with its own difficulties and challenges.

Some people may go even farther afield than seeking continuity or restitution. This attempt at recovering the past, conceptualized by Proust as "la recherche du temps perdu," encourages many to marry a person whom they knew in their youth, who failed to marry them then. Such marriages may be a phenomenon specific to our time, because people who were young in the 1930s frequently put off marriage until they had earned money, or until they had found a match which would better their position. This often meant that they did not marry the person with whom they first fell in love. And so, many people who are now old carry the dream or memory of their first love with them through the rest of their lives. Compared to their real spouse, whose inadequacies are revealed in the friction of daily living, the sweetheart of one's youth may, in fantasy, seem perfect in every way.

This problem may also face old people in the future. Today many people live together without getting married, and the institution of marriage has frequently been shown to be a shaky one. People now are often unsure whether they have found the right partner; they change lovers often in search of the "perfect" mate. By the time they marry, they may have abandoned many good, earlier choices. When they experience the difficulties and disappointments that marriage unavoidably entails, fantasies may blossom of how much better marriage would have been with the person whom one did not marry. This person from the past remains protected from the tests of reality and remains in memory as youthful, creative, and charming as he or she had been when they first met. The person whom one married, however, ages, and so does oneself.

It is probably true that bad marriages get worse and good marriages get better. Even good marriages, though, do not obliterate the emotional recall of the first love, remembered as these persons were in their youth. The French saying "on retourne toujours à ses anciens amours" (one always returns to one's old loves) refers to the greatest tragedies in second marriages. If, through widowhood or divorce, one is free to marry one's earlier love, and that person is available and responsive, fantasies are made the basis of reality. These old fantasies are likely to turn the new reality into disappointment and discomfort. A family home may still exist, but it has changed. The same people are there, but they have changed greatly as well. So neither fits the other. Spouses in the second marriage may present themselves publicly and, even more important, privately, as younger than they are, a stance which is both tragic and funny at the same time. To pretend like this is not to be "stoical" but to fight natural law. Hedonists would try to avoid hurt, and therefore would not become involved in such marriages. Existentialists, however, would counsel going ahead and experiencing marriage with the love of one's youth, or the person with whom one can "live out one's fantasies."

The problem which we are discussing in this chapter extends beyond second marriages. It applies to all marriages, however young the partners. The first object of one's love is one's mother and, throughout marriage, one cannot go back to her again. In our narcissistic age, our second love is probably ourselves. One cannot go back to the first love object, or find the mother in a wife or even less so in a husband. One also cannot go back to oneself as one was as a girl or boy or an infant. Obviously then, one cannot go back at age sixty or more to a childhood sweetheart or an adolescent love, because that person is now also probably past the sixty-year mark. The wisdom of Heraclitus says that "One cannot step twice into the same river." This applies to all issues of living. Life is an irreversible process; opportunity not used is opportunity lost.

In this context it is interesting to look at the problem of searching for the love of one's past from the viewpoint of Confucius. He said that "there are three things which the superior [person] guards against. In youth, when the physical powers are not yet settled, [one] guards against lust. When [one] is strong, and the physical powers are full of vigor, [one] guards against quarrelsomeness. When [one] is old, and the animal powers are decayed, [one] guards against covetousness." In other words, do not undertake what you are not fit for anymore; never mind your fantasies. Although we are not sure from this translation whether covetousness is meant in the sense of the Commandment "not to covet another man's wife," there is a strange ring of familiarity between Confucius and the Scriptures on this account.

Anybody who is obsessed with the thought of what might have been, is disabled from enjoying what can still be. One can never recapture what one has never captured. At the risk of destroying fantasies, which is unlikely, and at the risk of raising objections, which is probable, it is important to express these problems with regard to second marriages in which old people try to marry the embodiment of their first love.

The beloved may not have aged in one's memory, but he or she has aged in reality. The physical equipment for sexuality has gone downhill, or its decline may be very near in the future. Without the prop of sexuality, love is incomplete. It prevents the experience of wholeness which the heterosexual union implies. It precludes the experience of reproduction.

People who engage in such adventures are soon to make a discovery which Proust has beautifully described and which Simone de Beauvoir has referred to in *The Coming of Age*. Proust tells about his return to the Princesse de Guermantes' salon after an absence of many years. He has the impression that the host and the guests have disguised themselves, that the prince has provided himself with a white beard and, as it were, with leaden soles which dragged at his feet. He found a blonde girl made up "as a stout whitehaired lady."

When the illusion of a few weeks, months, or years wears off, the makeup of the beloved will be perceived and will be found to be reality. There is, however, a great difference between finding the signs of aging in a person with whom one has lived in a long marriage, and finding those same signs in a second marriage with somebody whom one imagines to be young. The bond created by a marriage between two young people is likely to endure in spite of the friction and difficulties which it will bring about over time. In a good marriage, as in good wine, aging improves quality. The physical signs of aging will evoke the response of tenderness in the other. In a bad marriage, the bad wine turns to vinegar. In an old-age marriage with the first beloved or the fantasy of him or her, there is less reason for tenderness and nurture, but there may be many reasons for the satisfaction of hatred, nourished by recurrent disappointments and the increase of unwelcome burdens. There is nothing but disappointment in trying to reverse the life cycle.

It should also be mentioned that in every marriage one becomes tied to a stranger, a stranger not only by sex but by development and genetic endowment. It takes a lot of time to reduce the strangeness and it takes even more time to accept its irreducible residue. Ultimately, every person guards some experiences and even more some wishes, wounds, and disappointments, conceivably even his or her victories, as part of oneself which he or she does not want to share. Partly, and probably frequently, this concealment may be caused by shame, partly by the power gained by withholding information, perhaps partly by a wish to spare the other. It can even occur — no one can venture to say how often — that in the union of the sex act, the partners conceal their fantasies from one another. As has been pointed out by Edrita Fried, no matter what the nature of such strangeness in marriage may be, it is made tolerable by familiarity and increasing renunciation of full knowledge. Whether residues of infantile sexuality should be dealt with in analysis or within the relationship, the element of time is of importance.

In our divorce-prone society many people do not give one another sufficient time to complete these adjustment processes. In old age, however, every remarriage suffers from a lack of time to make significant progress toward intimacy. To the strangeness of childhood and young adulthood which every marriage must cope with, has been added the strangeness of an adult life with which the old "newlyweds" are not intimately connected. The burden of strangeness therefore has increased and the time for reduction has decreased.

All remarriages in old age live also under the spectre of recall of the marriage partner whom one has lost through death or divorce. Now the relationship is reversed, the former marriage partner has disappeared. He or she is not here any more to annoy and to irritate one, and, if one was lucky, interactions with the first spouse were less and less annoying and irritating as time went on. The new marriage partner, however, is here to annoy and irritate now, and he or she is under unfair competition with somebody who has disappeared. If these deliberations are taken to be advice against remarriages between old people, they are doubly meant for remarriages of people who were in love and did not get married. Even if one of them should have stayed unmarried, that person may have cherished the love of his or her youth while becoming identified with a single life style. Women and men who have stayed unmarried until old age have probably lost the ability to give up the autonomy of singlehood which must be done in every marriage. Ultimately, old people are likely to get sick frequently, to become irritating by loss of hearing, to become crippled by arthritis, and finally to become terminal. One somehow endures these afflictions with a marriage partner of long standing. However, one can hardly help feeling imposed upon when one who was not married to another for the better part of their lives, begins to suffer disabling disease, or lingers on without hope. As one wise if not charitable widow said in a group discussion led by the senior author at a geriatric center, "nursing a terminal husband once" is enough.

10

Medical Intervention: Change of Consciousness and Hospitalization

The combination of the topics of change of consciousness and hospitalization in the same chapter may at first surprise the reader. However, medical prescription of substances which change consciousness and are used both in the hospital and at home are an established pattern of medical care for the aged. This is frequently overlooked or ignored, while the contemporary social scene is agitated by a condemnation of drug use by the young — and old. Medical practice and philosophical considerations actually oppose this blanket condemnation.

Change of consciousness through the use of substances such as wine, beer, hemp, and mescal has been known in many cultures and over all ages of history. They have found uses in religious practices and, therefore, were sanctioned rather than considered social evils. It is also known that wine, beer, and mead were used widely in antiquity and the Middle Ages. In fact, it is recorded that when Epicurus felt death was near, he ordered a bath and a bottle of wine, finished a letter, and died. What distinguishes drug use in modern times from drug use in the past is its use by young people for purposes of conformity, daring, show of courage, or escape.

It could also be said — probably with some justification — that never before in the history of civilization have so many parents and governmental agencies been willing to support young people in an idle life. The permissiveness of our culture and the lack of clear goal models have permitted many young people to evade the commitment to study or work and have deprived them of ego support which would prevent regressive anxieties and depression. Most parents do not see the connection between such consequences of their childrearing and the drug use of their children. Of course, a socially more productive way of keeping the regressive thought content of the unconscious from interfering with the process of growth is to gain input by learning, working, and relationships. We venture to say that the effect of these three factors is particularly strong during adolescence.

Through the development of pharmaceuticals and the easy import of drugs from other countries and continents, substances which lead to change of consciousness are in practically every medicine cabinet in the nation. From childhood on, children are acquainted with pain killers. In some school systems they are forced to take tranquilizers if they are unruly. In some youth-serving institutions, they are put on energizers. The underworld, through pushers, has invaded high schools and even grade schools. It would be an unusual child who could grow up in our culture without being exposed to the temptation to use drugs.

Similarly, the aged have learned to use drugs as part of a medical regimen prescribed by their physician. Pain killers and tranquilizers are a part of body and mind management of older persons. In case of hospitalization and surgery, they make life bearable for the patient. The memory of such relief is brought from the hospital to the nursing facility or home, and drug use is practiced there more or less with medical approval. In fact, it is frequently made possible by prescription.

The meaning of change of consciousness for the young and for the old, however, is different. For the young it is meeting a challenge, or bending to pressure to be like others, or escape from what seems to be intolerable internal conflict. Whatever its purpose, it is socially disapproved by the wider community and wastes time that could be used for the development of capacities for ego strength and for service to self and others. It is an expansive — but ultimately self-defeating — shortcut to feeling "right" within the world.

For many older people who must cope with the pains and disabilities of daily life, drug use is not waste, it is life management. In this form, drug use in moderation is approved at least by experienced and humanitarian physicians. Aging means losing: losing one's strength, one's influence, one's friends, one's spouse, and relatives. Not only the actual occurrence of these losses, but also their anticipation produces anguish and concern. Thus, anguish is always renewed because the bad news seems to bunch up, and one problem follows another in quicker and quicker succession as one approaches the end of the life span. One is reminded over and over again that the bad news does not stop. In consequence, one engages in anticipatory grief. One worries about the future of those for whom one feels responsible, in case one should die before them, and of course, one worries about oneself. We must therefore accept the existentialist formulation of death anxiety as dread of nothingness. This means the necessity of coping with anxiety, coping with bad news, and coping with sleeplessness and pain. One, and perhaps the most frequent, means of coping, is change of consciousness.

Perhaps the most urgent need for change of consciousness occurs during sleeplessness at night. If one is married and still shares a bedroom with one's spouse, one experiences a double bind between not waking one's spouse and wishing to find distraction through reading or watching television. Sometimes the situation becomes ironic. For example, when men with enlarged prostates are advised to void during the night so as to prevent bladder pressure upon the prostate, they must fully arouse themselves in order to leave the bedroom in darkness without bumping against something, walk gingerly, enter a dark bathroom, and return noiselessly. Having done so, and having returned to bed without waking one's spouse, one is likely to lie wide awake for hours, and the thoughts that will come are likely to be unpleasant. The enlarged prostate itself raises apprehension about the future need for surgical intervention. If one should die during surgery, the future of the spouse, particularly in times of inflation, may lead to financial worries. Her loneliness may give concern. One is likely to wonder who will take care of her when she gets ill, and one is — never mind Zenon and Epicurus — afraid of dying. It seems reasonable under such conditions that one should resort to sleeping pills.

These anxieties become even more pronounced for people who have suffered heart attacks or who have been found to have cancer. There is a difference between death anxiety before one has been up against death, and death anxiety afterwards. Of course, many people may deny or be deceived into believing that their tumors are not malignant and, for a while, this deception by themselves, or by others, may support them. With increasing information about cancer, the necessary follow-up examinations and the necessary post-operational treatments such as radiation, chemotherapy, and immunology make it exceedingly difficult to maintain either denial or reassurance. That one has had a heart attack cannot be concealed from the patient because of the regimen that he or she will have to observe. We live, therefore, in times where people know that they have brushed against death by disease and are likely to do so again. This produces an interesting shift from the delusion of immortality to the encounter with temporality. Again, tranquilizers, sleeping pills, and pain killers such as Demerol will come to the rescue of the person who is approaching death after having made an acquaintance with the likely killer. It is easier to die if one does not know or has not been forewarned about death. Readers may remember the legend as presented by Somerset Maugham in which Death is encountered in the marketplace and delivers a speech:

There was a merchant in Baghdad who sent his servant to market to buy provisions and in a little while the servant came back, white and trembling, and said, Master, just now when I was in the marketplace I was jostled by a woman in the crowd and when I turned I saw it was Death that jostled me. She looked at me and made a threatening gesture; now, lend me your horse, and I will ride away from this city and avoid my fate. I will go to Samarra and there Death will not find me. The merchant lent him his horse, and the servant mounted it, and he dug his spurs in its flanks and as fast as the horse could gallop he went. Then the merchant went down to the marketplace and he saw me standing in the crowd and he came to me and said, Why did you make a threatening gesture to my servant when you saw him this morning? That was not a threatening gesture, I said, it was only a start of surprise. I was astonished to see him in Baghdad, for I had an appointment with him tonight in Samarra.

A similar viewpoint with regard to the impact of drug use on the lives of the young and the old applies to the use of alcohol. For young people the use of alcohol can be the road to alcoholism and an essentially self-destructive life, destructive for spouse and children. Even if it does not lead to alcoholism, it may lead to the practice of changing consciousness in order to avoid coping with one's own conflicts, whatever they be. The use of alcohol may also be a means of seduction or a means of working up courage in sexual contacts. Finally, it is expensive and may bring about financial difficulties and career break-up.

The use of drugs and alcohol by the elderly, however, must be viewed in a different light. The dread of nothingness, of being diminished in social importance, of being threatened by painful diseases such as arthritis, or by terminal illness such as angina, and finally the concern for the survivor are all understandable reasons for change of consciousness by alcohol, as well as by drugs. From the viewpoint of Hedonism, it may well be acceptable. But from the viewpoint of Stoicism, it would be interfering with natural law. The existentialist might view it as a waste of potential. Retired persons are at no risk of losing a job, careers are not likely to be interrupted and relatives and spouse are likely to be more understanding with the use or abuse of alcohol or drugs by the old than by the young.

Even if drug use and use of alcohol should lead to addiction and alcoholism, these considerations would still hold to a certain degree. Few doctors worry whether a terminally ill cancer patient becomes a morphine addict, and this viewpoint could probably be extended to the social sphere of the alcoholic. It may be more respect-inspiring to face the burdens and impairments of old age stoically, but every principle can be carried to absurdity by application without discrimination. It should also be considered that in order to be stoical in the true sense of the word, one must have mental resources which permit the suffering of old age to be confronted with the dignity of maintained consciousness. For people without such resources it may be merciful and appropriate to grant them the privilege of change of consciousness in order to make their remaining time of life tolerable.

There is also a problem of the flux of time and the increase of physical and mental deterioration with advancing years that, through change of consciousness, may lead one from Stoicism or Existentialism to Hedonism as the age-appropriate philosophy. But it is important to consider the consequences of becoming addicted to either drugs or alcohol. It is only natural that some physicians who are committed to fighting drug abuse should become concerned about drug abuse in elderly persons. However, one must face the question of what the personal and social cost would be if a person in his or her seventies became addicted for such reasons. When simple pain killers do not work, and cancer begins to torture the body, when a patient after a heart attack becomes so fear-ridden that he or she begins to lead the existence of a vegetable, what is at stake if such a person becomes addicted? What usefulness to society or to the person is destroyed? Even if the addiction shortens life, does this not represent a relief for relatives, children, and spouses who must take care of such a person and, most of all, for the people themselves? Remember that Freud, when he felt that his life had become painful, disgusting to himself, and socially useless, asked Dr. Schur to help him to the end, and that Dr. Schur complied. This raises, then, an ultimate problem for the physician and the aged patient. One might well make the proposition that suicide is everybody's own business and that the burden should not be put on the physician. Recently the ethics of the problem have been stated so well that we cannot help but include in this chapter

the following quotation from Harold J. Wershow in
an article in *The Gerontologist:*

> Is it ethical to treat recurrent infections, such as pneu-
> monia, urinary tract infection, and the like, to deny
> their previous roles as the "old man's friends?" Must
> we be bound to keep alive as long as possible those
> poor souls who sit tied to their chairs babbling inco-
> herently, doubly incontinent, whose dining consists
> of having usually cold food stoked into them as rapid-
> ly as possible by overworked aides who must move
> on and stoke the next bed's prisoner? Is this living,
> much less living with dignity? We must realize that
> for every person, at some time, the moment arrives
> when *our* need to "do something" is inappropriate,
> even grotesque.

Unfortunately, hospitals are institutions geared to
"do something," and this presents special problems
to the aged patient and the hospital personnel. The
situation is complicated by the public nature of
everything that has or has not been done for the patient. Physicians, nurses, and technicians are all
under the social control of one another and, therefore, do not dare to omit something which theoreti-
cally, if inhumanly, could be done.

Although popular belief connects hospitals with
the idea of cure, popular practice uses hospitals frequently as places where one brings old people to
die, and defensive medicine by doctors who are apprehensive of malpractice suits frequently prolongs
the process. While in Western civilization attempts
are made to maintain the dying body, and to extend
life to the extreme of resuscitation of heart arrest,
intravenous feedings, and "iron lungs" which
breathe for people, the Nepalese people are more

purposeful in helping the dying to the end. They bring dying people to a special house next to the burning ghats. This house does not provide any curative efforts, but simply a waiting period until the old person dies. After having brought him or her to this spot they dunk the body in the water of the river, take the person back to the dying house, and then the whole family waits until death comes. Then the body is burned by a relative and the ashes swept into the water. Opposite the dying house on the other river bank there is a row of lingams which affirm fertility and the coming of new life. As mentioned before, the closest instance the authors know of connecting hospitals with dying in the West, is the location of the Veterans Hospital in Philadelphia, which is built adjacent to a cemetery. With almost equal clarity of understanding that hospitals are dying places, many funeral parlors in the West are closely situated to hospitals. The experience of dying in the hospital has come under frequent attack because the phenomenal development of medical technology has often made dying an experience of having a body connected with machinery; the body then fails the machinery, rather than vice versa. In some instances clinical death is simply dependent on the decision of physicians to let a patient die by disconnecting the machinery which maintains organic functioning. Since these developments have received wide publicity in the media, many old people know that when they are brought to the hospital in terminal condition, their autonomy over their existence and its length will be practically lost. This is also true for younger people who are hospitalized, but there the expectation is one of recovery and hope. In pediatrics, hospital personnel feel that they are supported by nature; in geriatrics, the feeling is one of a fight against natural law.

Of course, hope is long-lived and probably in many old people who are hospitalized in terminal condition there is also still some hope that they may recover, thanks to the miracles of modern medicine. Elizabeth Kubler-Ross has referred to this last flicker of hope in the five-stage dying process she has outlined. This attempt to hope by the terminal patient is classified as the first stage of "denial and isolation."

Certain amounts of well-being in old and terminally ill patients may be induced by spontaneous regression into infantile dependency and its pleasures. To be visited three times a day by a smiling young nurse, to be washed and, if necessary, fed by a woman of the age of one's mother when one was an infant may have its own gratifications which should not be underestimated by relatives or hospital staff. In a hospital one is also not alone. Physicians, nurses, aides, volunteers and visitors bring to the old people an amount of human contact that they may not have had for a long time. They may have to share a room with one or several patients, or even be in a ward where activity never ceases. In such situations input is brought to them far above what their life may have provided in the last years.

One of the primary gratifications of life is food, and unfortunately in hospitals it is notoriously bad. Patients and staff alike are miserably fed. Food is unimaginatively prepared and is cold when it is brought to the patient. One might wonder whether smaller expenditures for exotic machinery and greater allocation of funds to the provision and serving of palatable food might not be more humanitarian. Psychologically speaking, food is a symbol of love, and the quality of the hospital food can only suggest that it is a loveless place. In this symbolic context one can raise the question of how a person who is not loved can love oneself or others.

It is damaging to the self-image of many old patients that almost all doctors with whom they come into contact are younger and have authority over them. Sometimes this leads to the tactlessness of calling older patients by their first names. This may be meant as kindness but is very likely to give offense. It is made doubly rankling and hurtful because few patients dare to antagonize their doctors by insisting on being called by their title or full name. Certainly the word "Mr." or "Mrs." or "Miss" should never be absent from the address of a patient by a member of the health care team. This is, however, only one aspect of a much larger phenomenon of dehumanization which the old must suffer in hospitals and institutions for the aged. Jules Henry says, in an article about personality and aging, that old people are subjected to "depersonalization through symbolic means — especially the generalized loss of communication possibilities and the negative handling of the body; depersonalization through material means — essentially the deprivation of the material amenities, the generally poor quality of the available material culture, and the use of material objects in a distorted way; depersonalization through extinction or violation of shame and disgust functions; depersonalization through routinization and deprivation of individuality and protection; depersonalization through inconstancy and distortion of the human environment; and depersonalization through staff self-centeredness."

There is also a special process of deceptively sparing communication which tells patients bad news only slowly, partially, and in ever-increasing doses, thereby giving the patient a feeling of a succession of bad news which in itself is emotionally damaging, and which can lead to despair. First they are informed that they must have tests, then they may have to be put on intravenous feedings, then perhaps that they will have to be treated for an inflammation, then further that they will have to be treated for a malignancy. The description of the operation and the discomforts attached to it is usually sketchily and reluctantly given. After the operation they may be informed that there may be a need for chemotherapy because the cancer had been found to be too far advanced, or that they may need radiation.

The patient is, therefore, never fully prepared for the next stage of the process of either medical intervention or, finally, for the process of dying. Again the old person is treated like a child who cannot understand, who cannot confront fate, and who cannot make the decision on how he or she wants to die, whether attached to machinery produced by medical technology, or at home with retention of the old self but perhaps after a shorter period of time. It should be considered, however, that dying at home may put a burden of actual work and a stimulation of death anxiety on the family members which may defeat its own purpose. It is perfectly possible that patients who die in the hospital or in an institution may do so in a more restful environment than their home can provide. Still, even in hospitals and institutions there is no guarantee of peace.

Although it would be desirable to propose a strategy for the choice of a dying place (home, hospital, or institution) which could be used as a guideline in all cases, the authors feel that the decision must be left with those who "foot the bill." Some people will find caring for the dying at home emotionally satisfying, the fulfillment of an ethical obligation and an act of love. Others may find it frightening, physically and emotionally draining, and an experience connecting their home with a persistent remembrance of the corpse of the departed as well as a reminder of their own mortality. Some people will find the knowledge of the death of a loved one in a hospital a lasting source of guilt and an ultimate rejection of somebody whom they should have stood by until the end. We must also mention that frequent visits to the hospital or institutional bedside of the dying is physically exhausting and emotionally taxes one's limits. The general trend of our culture toward the medicalization of all major life events frequently takes the problem of decision-making out of the realm of individual choice and makes hospitals and institutions the generally accepted dying places for most people.

The greatest burden of old patients is not worry about themselves, or how to cope with the anxiety of dying, but concern about spouses and children; this is particularly true when these people show that they are upset, thus adding considerable burden to the difficulties of being hospitalized and conceivably terminal. To the burden of being sick, physically in pain or uncomfortable, is added the burden of pacifying the anticipatory mourners, worrying about their future, and somehow feeling imposed upon that so close to the end one should still have to think about others. Therefore, we must come to the conclusion that our culture as yet provides no standards of care which would secure the dignity and peacefulness of dying. The general need for an etiquette for aging, which we mentioned earlier, finds its most poignant expression here.

It has often been said that patients in modern hospitals need an advocate, but when an upset spouse or relative assumes that function and begins to question treatment procedures, diets, and nursing care, the patients are really in a double bind. They know that their advocates mean well and may even be right, but they depend on their physicians, on residents, nurses, and aides more than on their advocates. If hospital staff are irritated by the advocate, the patient is forced to play the mediator by showing appreciation for the efforts of the advocate, and by placating those whom the advocate may have offended.

Another burden which old patients often do not know how to cope with are visitors who come unannounced, who do not ask whether the patient is ready to receive them, who stay too long, and who force the patient into the role of the host which the patient is often too weak and uncomfortable to perform. With a physical appearance which is felt to be a disagreeable sight to the visitors, an overburdened person is placed into a social role which in many instances serves the visitors better than the patient. The visitors feel that they have done their share in showing compassion, fulfilling social obligations, or in having done what expresses their gratitude for not having to be in the patient's place.

Some therapists have found that touch is more comforting and strengthening than talk. One would be tempted to suggest that touch visits should take the place of talk visits. The friendly human touch of a loved one or a friend who is holding one's hand or sitting by the bedside is comforting without putting the patient under the obligation of active response. One should also remember that old people frequently suffer a loss of hearing and do not always understand what their visitors say. They must strain to understand, and they undergo even further strain by being polite and attempting to answer what they have not understood.

Still and all, many old patients who do not die are reluctant to leave the hospital because they have no place to go. They are now in a position in which they are unable to care for themselves and fear, rightfully, a demeaning existence in an old age home. Relatives and spouses may not be able to resume the care of the old person that discharge requires. Dimly or clearly, the old persons feel that, although they are reduced to the status of a child in the hospital, they are at least cared for. Unfortunately hospitals are anxious to free their beds for new patients. Utilization committees keep track of patients for whom no further medical help promises improvement. Every social service department in the hospital is likely to have a list of problem cases of this nature, people who are not expected to die immediately but for whom no medical help seems to promise results. Convalescent home space may not be available, at least at prices which the patients or their relatives can afford, and so we find a special minority of old people in hospitals, the unwanted who do not want to go to an old age home, or for whom no such home is available. It is remarkable that patients want to stay in the hospital where they are not wanted because the exchange principle, in its immediate and in its most powerful form, does not work. The patient has little to give to the nursing staff, hardly anything acceptable to the resident, and perhaps a few dollars to an aide. These gifts by patients or relatives must come into play, however, in order to give the encounter between health care personnel and patients the personal touch which concretizes a relationship.

In fairness to the hospital one must state that the incurable and the dying patients represent great burdens intellectually and emotionally for hospital personnel. To the physician, the death of a patient proves ultimate defeat in what society expects and what deep in his or her heart the physician probably expects, too, namely that he or she will be a successful fighter with death. To the nurse the preparation of the corpse for removal from the room to the basement of the hospital is a difficult and probably emotionally frightening task. The very fact of transportation of the shrouded body of what was a patient and is now a corpse from a hospital floor to the basement may also be made difficult by concern that the other patients will notice what is being transported there. However, although the task of preparing a dead patient for transfer to a funeral parlor may be disagreeable, it doesn't provide the same narcissistic wound that the death of a patient inflicts upon the doctor. The nurse has not been responsible for curing the patient, neither by training, nor by social expectation. The responsibility is put on the physician, and this responsibility ultimately cannot be met, no matter what defenses doctors may develop against the anxiety about failing as physicians when their patients die. It is the tragedy of medicine and suggests a divisional function. Terminal patients should not be the responsibility of the physician. They should be in the care of nurses who have not the mandate of maintaining life, and who therefore, will not have to suffer the same ego damage that doctors ultimately suffer when their patients die. It may also make possible the abandonment of affective neutrality which doctors feel, and frequently practice. If one is responsible for patients and feels it on an individuial basis, and if one permits oneself to develop a relationship, then the death of a patient is a part of one's personal experience. It occurs repetitively and cannot be borne. Since nurses have only the responsibility of care, but not the responsibility of cure, they probably are better equipped than physicians to provide for the final period in a person's life, in terms of support and attention.

11

Coping Through Transcendence

For better or worse people identify their existence with what is surrounded by their skin. Actually it is only this exterior of the body which they know reasonably well, and they know more about their front than they know about their back. Other people similarly identify us by our outward appearance, particularly by the texture and structure of our faces. They frequently deduce the quality of our mental and emotional life from the appearance of our faces. We assume therefore that there is harmony between the interior and exterior; we are surprised when a beautiful person exhibits a nasty temperament and, equally so, when a homely person shows beauty of mind and emotions. Our body exterior shows visible and increasing deterioration with advancing years. Tissues become flaccid, crowsfeet appear around the eyes, lesions appear, the whole body loses its shapeliness and, toward the end, it becomes bent over and frequently crippled with arthritis. Since other people tend to equate our mind with our body, they often suspect that our mind and emotions are also deteriorating with the years. There may well be some justification for this suspicion, because it is difficult to experience one's own external deterioration without getting angry about it, mourning one's loss of vigor and attractiveness, and suffering wounds to one's self-image. Grooming and subtle adjustments in clothing may help but they cannot prevent the change in appearance of one's face and body, reminding us of our approach to nothingness.

In these medically sophisticated times we also have some awareness that we are changing internally. We are reminded by our physicians that our arteries are narrowing, that our bone structure is becoming brittle. Men are reminded that their prostate glands are growing, women are instructed to examine their breasts for tumors and to undergo pelvic examinations which may reveal malignancies.

It is, therefore, one of the problems of aging to cope with an increasing awareness of external and internal deterioration of the body. It has been suggested by a professor of psychology, Robert Peck, that the true adjustment to aging must encompass a transcendence of the body, of work, and of self to cope with these changes and with the increasing awareness of our approach to death. His formulations are so perfect that we have decided to quote them rather than to paraphrase them.

> *Work Transcendence* . . . The chief issue might be put this way: "Am I a worthwhile person only insofar as I can do a full time job; or can I be worthwhile in other, different ways — as a performer of several other roles, and also because of the kind of person I am?"
>
> The process of ego-differentiation into a complex, varied set of self-identifications begins in early childhood. There are reasons, however, for considering it a centrally important issue at the time of vocational re-

tirement. For most men, the ability to find a sense of self-worth in activities beyond the "job" seems to make the most difference between a despairing loss of meaning in life, and a continued, vital interest in living. (For many women, this stage may arrive when their "vocational" role as mother is removed by the departure of the grown children. In that case, this crisis-stage might well come in middle age, for many women.)

There is an even broader issue at stake, however. For most Americans, at least, vocational retirement means a sharp reduction in income. This means a reduced standard of living, with all of the sense of depreciation of status symbols and worth-symbols this may entail. Another consequence is that many retired people must adjust to a new state of dependence on others, in sharp contrast with their decades-long experience of being self-sufficient and self-supporting. If this enforced shift is to be met successfully, it requires ego-differentiation of a different kind: not just differentiation among varied role activities, but among different attributes of personality and interpersonal relationship. Thus, the person who has built his self-respect primarily on the value of rugged independence may see nothing left to live for when he can no longer fulfill this part of his make-up. On the other hand, a man or woman who finds meaningful satisfaction in being a "good friend" to people, in sensual pleasures of sunning, swimming, or "just sitting," or in some other side of his nature, mayh positively welcome retirement as an opportunity to develop these other aspects of life more fully.

Body Transcendence vs. Body Preoccupation. Old age brings to almost everyone a marked decline in resistance to illness, a decline in recuperative powers, and increasing experience with bodily aches and pains.

For people to whom pleasure and comfort mean predominantly physical well-being, this may be the gravest and most mortal of insults. There are many such people whose elder years seem to move in a decreasing spiral, centered around their growing preoccupation with the state of their bodies.

There are other people, however, who suffer just as painful physical unease, yet who enjoy life greatly. It may be that these are people who have learned to define "happiness" and "comfort" more in terms of satisfying human relationships, or creative activities of a mental nature, which only sheer physical destruction could seriously interfere with. In their value system, social and mental sources of pleasure and self-respect may transcend physical comfort, alone.

Ego Transcendence vs. Ego Preoccupation. One of the new and crucial facts of old age is the appearance of the certain prospect of personal death. In earlier years death comes unexpectedly, as it were; but elderly people know it must come. Chinese and Hindu philosophers, as well as Western thinkers, have suggested that a positive adaptation is possible, even to this most unwelcome of prospects. The constructive way of living the late years might be defined in this way: To live so generously and unselfishly that the prospect of personal death — the night of the ego, it might be called — looks and feels less important than the secure knowledge that one has built for a broader, longer future than any one ego ever could encompass. Through children, through contributions to the culture, through friendships — these are ways in which human beings can achieve enduring significance for their actions which goes beyond the limit of their own skins and their own lives. It may, indeed, be the only *knowable* kind of self-perpetuation after death.

Such an adaptation would not be a stage of passive resignation or of ego-denial. On the contrary, it requires deep, active effort to make life more secure, more meaningful, or happier for the people who will go on after one dies. Since death is the one absolute certainty for all people, this kind of adaptation to its prospect may well be the most crucial achievement of the older years.

Although we identify with Peck's philosophy of transcendence, we believe that it was formulated without regard to cases of extremely painful diseases and very advanced old age, an area to which we will soon return. Ideally, Peck's concepts seem not only to offer a philosophical solution that shows the wisdom and power of detachment from something that one is going to lose. They may also, if achievable, come as close to harmony with natural law as a human being may be able to come. There are, however, certain concrete obstacles to this attainment. Outstanding among them are disabling pain and decrease in function, such as heavy breathing with exertion, difficulties in voiding, and arthritic pains in joints. Recurrent pain and increasing loss of functinal capacities are permanent stimuli to becoming self-concerned, to dwelling on one's discomforts and to mourning the passing of a better pain-free time. In a grim paradox, that body from which one wants to detach oneself attaches itself with ever more insistent demands for one's attention. The body is not a philosopher, and detachment from an aging body is an increasingly difficult task. It is as if the mind, set upon detachment, were always tripped up by the body in which it must dwell.

There have, of course, been cultures in which a refusal to yield to pain, or even the experience of pain as a part of religious services, has been required. The American Plains Indians are said to have extolled the sufferin of pain as heroic human virtue. Peck's concept of the transcendence of the body and its deterioration is, interestingly, part of the Catholic tradition. The pious Catholic offers his or her suffering as a gift to God and thereby finds meaning in the deterioration of the body. C.S. Lewis writes, "If pain sometimes shatters the creature's false self-sufficiency, yet in supreme 'Trial' or 'Sacrifice' it teaches him the self-sufficiency which really ought to be his — the strength, and that alone, which God confers upon his subjected will." For most of us who are not blessed with such an ideological support system, pain is an increasing nuisance which sometimes grows into torture, and which is experienced as loss rather than spiritual gain.

The loss of work connected in our society with retirement is similarly something which we are supposed to extol. As mentioned in another context, compulsory retirement is much decried in our society. It seems, however, that people find it easier to transcend the loss of work than the loss of an attractive and well-functioning body. Very few people who are recalled from retirement are anxious to go back to work, and many find that it is just the deterioration of their bodies which makes the loss of work an adjustment rather than an additional hardship. After a period of upset and possible depression, most retired people settle down to life on a reduced scale which they can just manage with the vitality and residuial functioning still available to them.

Shopping, keeping the house clean, taking care of the yard, going to the doctor for checkups, resting when one is tired, paying bills, telephoning friends, making errands and tending to one's finances, consume so much time for a slowed-down body that retirement is often experienced as a life saver rather than as hurtful. It may be well to remember that people start a life without work and that retirement in a way permits them to return to the state in which they have started. It must also be considered that in a period of rapid change very few people attain retirement age without an inkling of having become obsolete,of barely holding on, and of not even knowing what their younger associates know and put to use. Most of all, retirement releases one from daily contact with the would-be successors and thereby from reminders that it is time to go. Perhaps even more important in our times is the concept of authenticity in work. With the adoption of the division of labor in manufacturing and also in professional work, such as in medical care or in the practice of law, few people identify with the results of their work as something specifically their own. Most types of work have stopped being creative. The process of work has become depersonalized and is therefore frequently carried out without any sense of fulfillment or essentiality to one's own well-being. The frequent changes of work that people in our time attempt in their search for authenticity testifies to this condition. In essence, therefore, retirement may well be liberation rather than eviction in many instances. If it were not for its economic implications, it would be an easy experience for many. Even with its economic effects, it seems to be reasonably managed by the anonymous people who do not send representatives to demonstrate or to testify before committees of the Senate. By contrast with the transcendence of the body, transcendence of work seems therefore an easy task of aging. Ultimately it is not giving up something but adjusting something to the more demanding task of life maintenance in the here and now.

Transcendence of the self is, of course, the opposite of the threat of nothingness. It implies the acceptance of one's own relative insignificance, and it would probably be unacceptable to most of us. It implies giving up the pursuit of one's own self-interest in the service of others, be they other people, movements, or ideas. Even the idea of altruism, or more strongly expressed, the idea of self-sacrifice, requires the belief that what one gives up is worthwhile. It is, therefore, a contradiction to say that one should give up something because it is not worth having, but it may be worthwhile for something else. In practical terms old people are exhorted not to be a burden on their children, not to frighten their associates by their own misery, and to devote themselves to causes on the communal or wider level. All these may be worthwhile uses of the self, but they are not transcendence of self.

We are coming, then, to the question whether transcendence of body, work, and self are really adjustment in old age or extremely difficult psychological demands which many people will either disregard or fail to meet. Unless one dies a sudden death it is much more likely that the impossibility of transcending a painful body and an unsatisfactory self will lead to a solution which is not transcendence but combat or abandonment. It is the senior author's deepest conviction that many people die because they do not want to live any more. They may have simply become too tired to continue the effort of living under the blows of fate. Or they may give up the struggle with pain and incapacitation. It is, of course, true that a sense of obligation toward others may lead people to put up with pain much longer than they would do for themselves, but ultimately they will stop cooperating with life-maintaining support systems. They will either stop eating adequate food or they will not cooperate with the hospital; they will turn to the wall, as it were, and wish to be left alone. In some sense this is by no means a sad ending. It is the final assertion of autonomy over one's own life, a last experience of power on the part of the powerless. Having no choice in coming into existence, they at least have a choice about staying in it. In such a way dying is an exercise of power rather than a submitting to it. Seeing it from this point of view, suicide — however oblique — becomes a dignified response to having been born.

12

The Meaning of Wisdom in Aging: The Harvest

Wisdom has always been regarded as a reward of aging. In ancient times when very few people lived the full three-score-and-ten, people who had an opportunity to accumulate experience over seventy years appeared to be superior to younger people in understanding the challenges of living. They seemed to have more know-how in coping with difficulty and to be in possession of solutions to problems which left younger people bewildered and undecided. With more and more people reaching the full life span, these exceptional characteristics of old age have become less valuable. Even worse, because of the rapidity of social change in technology and life style, experience seems useless in helping the young to solve their problems.

This somewhat sober picture is misleading, however, because it fails to distinguish the people for whom the wisdom of the aged has practical significance. In historical perspective one is likely to assume that it is the young who should profit from the accumulated experience of the aged. In modern times it is more important to explore whether the wisdom of the aged can profitably apply to the solution of the problems with which the aged themselves are faced. If one wants to insist, however, that accumulated wisdom should not only be age-specific but applicable to all ages, one would have to assume that the wisdom of the aged can be made desirable to the young by providing them with a perspective in addition to that which their experiences provide. One might visiualize an old person and a young person strolling in the same landscape and exchanging their impressions from their different angles of perceiving and reflecting.

The definition of wisdom as the accumulation of experience makes wisdom a relative concept. The extent of wisdom is the extent of understanding that has been derived from the different qualities of experience. It can be presumed that, in general, added years will mean added experience. It is not certain, however, that added experience means added reflection. People can run from experience to experience, or they can be bombarded by situation after situation without taking time out, or without having the capacity to reflect and to gather the meaning from what is happening to them, and from what they see happening to others. One might therefore be tempted to say that wisdom can be acquired only by persons who take time out to reflect on what has happened. Unfortunately, most people do not reflect on what has happened, but dwell in their thoughts on what they hope will happen. Since nobody knows what will happen, this type of thought work is likely to be unproductive. it could be productive only in rare cases where people by chance or by superior powers of analysis can conclude from the past and the present what the future will be.

In our egalitarian society it is easier to benefit from the experience of peers than from the experience of superiors or inferiors. It would follow, therefore, that the advisors of the young will be more effective if they are young, and the advisors of the old more effective if they are old themselves. That this cannot be applied in most instances of professional help is, of course, obvious, because it would lead to intolerable segregation of helpers and people to be helped. In practical terms, the advice of the old will benefit the young only if the young request it, not when it is offered without having been asked for. Similarly the advice which the young have to give to the old will have to be requested. In other words, every age group has wisdom that the other age group may need, but it can be conveyed only upon request.

An additional difficulty lies in the frequently observed phenomenon that the meaning of experience cannot be conveyed fully to the person who has not had similar experiences. Except for those people who suffer under what psychiatrists call a repetition compulsion, or have developed their character as a defense, old people are likely to have learned from their experience what they are not equipped to do. Wisdom implies a recognition of limits and not only of limits for self, but also limits for others. When this is conveyed to young people, it is of course unlikely to be accepted. To convey the wisdom of recognizing limitations might be of great assistance, however, to old people who have failed to see the limits brought upon them by an aging body, an aging mind, aging associates, and diminishing time.

As mentioned previously, the wisdom of the aged includes recognizing that the old are poor prospects for adequate exchanges with younger people. There is simply not enough time for people in their seventies to plan and execute exchanges with people in their thirties. Younger people may find it easier to see that. For old people it requires the acceptance of reaching the end of life. They may be tempted, therefore, to think in terms of a longer relationship to younger people than reality will permit. Wisdom of the aged demands an understanding of the time perspective of the young. We have touched upon that in general terms in Chapter IV in the discussion of the exchange principle in families, and also in Chapter VIII in the discussion of the dangers and disappointments which are likely to occur when old people remarry.

It would appear that the wisdom of old age is not to expect rewards for what they have done for others in the past. What they can expect from the young in reciprocity must be related to what they have to give in the present or in the future. Nonmaterial rewards which sons and daughters appreciate would be attempts by the old to understand their behavior, interest in their success without regard for the differences in social values, and giving the next generation the benefit of the doubt. Most importantly, old people might make themselves available when needed and not use their discomforts as weapons of hostility. Material rewards may more frequently express themselves after one is dead.

Another experience of advancing years which borders on wisdom or is perhaps wisdom itself, lies in the recognition that one can change others only by changing oneself. This wisdom unfortunately is rarely found in the aged, because as one gets older, one becomes more set in one's ways and more likely to disregard the fact that the passing of time means changed conditions to which old reactions and responses do not apply anymore. Nothing is more pathetic than an old liberal who appears to his young associates to be an arch conservative. A German poet, Friedrich Hebbel, had one of his heroes remark that the world had fallen asleep over its old victories. Not to fall asleep over one's old victories is probably one of the hardest tasks of wisdom in old age. Body and mind get tired, and it is difficult not to accept the invitation to rest on one's laurels.

What one may also have learned in old age is that in the aging period doing more for others than one can expect in return will keep one in contact with the world and protect a person from loneliness. Egotism is always a poor maker of friends, but it is particularly ineffective in old age. Similarly people must not wait for others to come to them when they are old; it is better to take the initiative than to find out that others did not take it. Loneliness is a terrible thing and the most terrible thing of all is that in old age it is frequently self-made. One could therefore claim wisdom for those aged who maintain themselves in the network of human relationships through initiative, generosity, and expectation of little in return.

Perhaps the greatest attainment of wisdom in old age is not to quarrel with the fact that one's children have not fulfilled all one's expectations and fantasies, that they have married someone whom one would have preferred not to see them marry, or that they have remained childless when one wanted grandchildren. The complaint that they do not visit as often as one might wish them to, or that they have not achieved financial or professional success, is doomed to failure. The fact that they lead lives which in one's own time might have been considered pathological or immoral is difficult but necessary to bear. Although the different social classes may differ in their expression of this parental disappointment, it is a pervasive and timeless phenomenon of parenting. Children rarely carry out the fantasies of their parents. Giving up those fantasies, and not connecting anger with renunciation is a great and wise achievement.

So far we have been concerned with wisdom in relationship to others. In summary, wisdom is the ability to learn from the young; it is the capacity to recognize limitations; it is a continued awareness and practice of the exchange principle in relation with others; it is creativity in the avoidance of loneliness; and, finally, it is the acceptance of belonging to an earlier culture in the flux of history.

It is now important to turn to that part of wisdom which covers the relationship with oneself. Aging people lead diminishing lives. Vitality and body vigor go down, hearing and eyesight lose their sharpness, arthritis affects body posture, medically prescribed diets diminish the range of eating pleasures, insomnia shortens one's sleep, memory fails, and pain and fatigue become constant companions. One must learn to live with these various facets of a diminishing life without anger; forgetting the name of a person of whom one is thinking, not liking one's picture in the mirror, are all aspects of aging. Not to be able to do what formerly one was able to do is not one's mistake. The decline of old age is as natural as the growth of youth. Since we all know that growth has been painful, it certainly would not be wise to expect that decline should be free of pain.

One speaks very much of permissiveness in the rearing of children. One might with better justification advocate permissiveness with self in declining years. Here philosophy comes into conflict with medicine. The aged need not accept the professional viewpont of the physician who values prolongation of life versus quality of life. It is the individual who must determine whether to stay within the boundaries set by professional health care workers or not.

Of course these diminishing capacities require ever renewed adaptation. One must learn to wear eyeglasses or braces, one must learn to come closer to people in order to hear, and one must not be tempted to pretend that one has understood when one has not, or to have seen when one has not. One must permit oneself more frequent rest and one must become satisfied with unfinished tasks.

Most of all, as mentioned previously, one must learn to bear one's diminishments so that others do not become frightened by them. One must not engage in a pattern of suppressing facts about one's condition, and by this, give people the fear of the unknown. One can type while having arthritis, one can do full professional work while being in chemotherapy for cancer; not all productivity is dependent on mobility. Heart patients can still work and love. Probably the happiest retirement recorded in history was that of Lucius Cornelius Sulla who, after having been the dictator of Rome, spent the years after abdication of his office with dancers, singers, actors and women, and in writing his memoirs. With these conditions one can still be host or guest or empathic friend, and can enjoy food and drink. In any case, one must prove to the world that even serious disease does not need to be disabling or a terror to one's associates. To failure can be added laughter, to loss, the dignity of bearing. As every comfort has its own discomfort, so one will find that every discomfort has its own comfort, too. Fatigue makes rest not only a necessity, but a delight. Adjustment of eyeglasses improves one's sight, hearing aids, if one can tolerate them, are a great victory over deafness.

Ultimately, in old age one will find comfort in what life should have taught everybody earlier. Good days follow bad days, and bad days follow good days, no matter what one does; the victory lies in survival and quitting when one is ahead. The essential stupidity in old age is the refusal to step down, and the resentment of those who want to step into one's place, as if anybody would be willing for another's sake to accept his or her own stagnation.

At one point or another in time, the changes of old age will require giving up part of one's autonomy in acting. This can only be resisted at great peril. Old people who want to climb ladders and make financial decisions of major consequence will find themselves with broken legs and broken fortunes. The ultimate wisdom of aging, therefore, is to diminish the expectations of self in relation to one's diminishing faculties. Wisdom is harmony between oneself as one is or has become, and the world as it is and has become.

There is one more problem calling for wisdom in aging, and that is coming to terms with one's impending death. Many philosophers have focused on this particular problem without finding a convincing answer. The philosophical stance has usually been that death is part of natural law and that, as a natural event, it needs neither to be feared nor resisted. Stoicism and Hedonism agree on this point and deny the meaning and terror of death, while existentialism derives from death the meaning of existence and makes the threat of nothingness a cornerstone of its system. The real answer, as has been mentioned, is that the increasing burden of a diminished and painful life eventually turns the will to live into a will to die. Some people terminate their lives by omission of life-sustaining activities rather than by a direct act of suicide. They seem to give up the will to live, to lose interest in others, to refuse to respond to the visits of friends, and they die sooner than would be expected from a physiological point of view. This could be called "implicit suicide" because omission of life-sustaining activities seems to be the only method by which old people in their existential despair can put their will to die into effect. A famous example of this is the tea and toast diet of the "old and alone."

Several conclusions suggest themselves in this context. Wisdom implies the power to evaluate specific situations in terms of general principles. One of these principles is the preference of quality over quantity of life. Another one is not to demand of time more hope than it has to give. And, ultimately, a part of wisdom is knowing when to stop.

Suggested Readings

Anderson, Joan E. ed., *Psychological Aspects of Aging* (Washington, D.C.: American Psychological Assocaiation, 1956).

Beard, Belle Boone, *Social Competence of Centenarians* (Athens, GA: University of Georgia Printing Department, 1967).

Berezin, Martin A. and Cath, Stanley H. eds., *Geriatric Psychiatry: Grief, Loss and Emotional Disorders in the Aging Process* (New York: International Universities Press, Inc., 1965).

Carp, Frances M. ed., *The Retirement Process,* Report of a Conference December, 1966, Gaithersburg, Maryland (Washington: U.S. Government Printing Office, 1967).

Cumming, Elaine and Henry, William E. *Growing Old: The Process of Disengagement,* (New York: Basic Books, 1961).

de Beauvoir, Simone, *The Coming of Age* (New York: G.P. Putnam's Sons, Inc., 1972).

Harris, Louis & Associates, Inc. *The Myth and Reality of Aging in America,* (Washington, 1975).

Kimmel, Douglas C. *Adulthood and Aging,* (New York: John Wiley & Sons, Inc., 1974).

Kubler-Ross, Elizabeth *Questions and Answers on Death and Dying,* (New York: MacMillan, 1974).

Lewis, Clives Staples *The Problem of Pain,* 11th Printing (New York: MacMillan Company, 1971).

Lopata, Helena Z. *Widowhood in an American City,* (Cambridge, Mass: Schenkman, 1973).

McKinney, John C. and de Vyver, Frank T. eds., *Aging and Social Policy, (New York: Appleton-Century-Crofts, 1966).*

Neugarten, Bernice L. and Havighurst, Robert J. eds., Social Policy, Social Ethics and the Aging Society, (University of Chicago: Committee on Human Development, 1976).

Neugarten, Bernice L. ed., *Middle Age and Aging,* (Chicago: The University of Chicago Press, 1968).

Pollak, Otto and Wise, Ellen S. *Invitation to a Dialogue: Union and Separation in Family Life,* (S.P. Medical & Scientific Books, a Division of Spectrum Publications, Inc., 1979).

Riley, Matilda W. and Foner, Anna *Aging and Society, Volume*

I: An Inventory of Research Findings (New York: Russell Sage Foundation, 1968).

Sarason, Seymour B. *Work, Aging and Social Change* (Riverside, N.J.: The Free Press, 1977).

Shanas, Ethel ed., *American Behavioral Scientist,* 14:1 (1970).

_____, *The Health of Older People: A Social Survey* (Cambridge: Harvard University Press, 1962).

Ethel Shanas et al., *Old People in Three Industrial Societies* (New York: Atherton Press, 1968).

Tibbits, Clark and Donahue, Wilma *Social and Psychological Aspects of Aging* (New York: Columbia University Press, 1962).

Tunstall, Jeremy *Old and Alone: A Sociological Study of Old People* (London: Routledge and Kegan Paul, 1966).

Woodruff, Diana S. and Birren, James E. *Aging: Scientific Perspectives and Social Issues* (New York: D. Van Nostrand Company, 1975).